Primer of Methods for the Behavioral Sciences

Primer of Methods for the Behavioral Sciences

Robert Rosenthal
Harvard University

Ralph L. Rosnow
Temple University

JOHN WILEY & SONS, Inc.
New York · London · Sydney · Toronto

Library of Congress Cataloging in Publication Data:

Rosenthal, Robert, 1933–
  Primer of methods for the behavioral sciences.

  Bibliography: p.
  1. Social sciences—Methodology. 2. Psychology—Methodology. I. Rosnow, Ralph L., joint author.
II. Title.
H61.R67   300'.1'8   73–18295
ISBN 0-471-73676-7
ISBN 0-471-73675-9 (pbk.)

Printed in the United States of America

10-9 8 7 6 5 4 3 2 1

To Mary Lu and Mimi

preface

This primer is a brief introduction to research methods and strategies in the behavioral sciences. It is not intended to produce experienced researchers but wiser students and consumers of behavioral research. We hope that it will be useful not only in a variety of undergraduate courses in the behavioral sciences but also to professionals who are not scientists—attorneys, businessmen, and journalists, for example.

We have pretested sections of the book with undergraduate students in several courses, with graduate students looking for a brief review, and with adult extension students enrolled in occasional courses but not necessarily pursuing any degrees. The favorable feedback from these groups prompted us to complete the book. Although most of the material is elementary, we hope there are some things that will interest even the instructor of the course. Thus, the method of standardizing the margins is not yet generally known to behavioral scientists but is important.

Our practical experience as researchers has benefited enormously over the years from the support of the Division of Social Sciences of the National Science Foundation, our respective universities, the Australian-American Educational Foundation, the Guggenheim Foundation, and from the efforts of Freed Bales, Hilde Himmelweit, Robert Lana, and Brendan Maher.

We thank the American Association for the Advancement of Science and the American Psychological Association for permission to reprint figures and other copyright data.

We are grateful to Donna DiFurio and Mari Tavitian for their devoted and expert typing. And, finally, we thank Paul Holland, David Kenny, David Rosenthal, and Frank J. Kohout for their helpful suggestions for the improvement of the book. However, if there are errors, we alone are responsible for them.

Robert Rosenthal
Ralph L. Rosnow

contents

chapter one

behavioral science and the structure of discovery

WHAT IS BEHAVIORAL SCIENCE?

There are so many fields of inquiry, or disciplines, that involve the study of behavior that it has become convenient to lump them all together under the heading of The Behavioral Sciences. The behavior of early man, political man, economic man, man as a social animal, man as a speaker, and man as a logician is the concern of psychologists, anthropologists, political scientists, economists, linguists, biologists, specialists in communication and education, and mathematicians. For most purposes it probably does not matter much whether one can distinguish among the various disciplines comprising the behavioral sciences. However, when some purpose can be served by making a distinction, there are several criteria available.

Each of the behavioral sciences has a body of theory, concepts, data, and methods of inquiry that make it possible, on the whole, to distinguish it from other, related fields. When a behavioral scientist draws heavily on the theoretical orientations and methods of more than one field, he is called an interdisciplinarian. If there are enough workers who find a very similar combination of theory, concepts, data and methods useful, the labeling problem is solved by inventing a new discipline. Examples of new disciplines in the behavioral sciences are mathematical psychology, neuropsychology, sociolinguistics, psychochemistry, behavioral genetics, psychological anthropology, psychopharmacology, psychophysiology, and social psychology. Most of these boundary-melting disciplines are of recent origin. Behavioral scientists hope that the new fields, by virtue of their synthesizing properties, will show the same hybrid vigor and potential for breakthrough found in the combination of formerly differentiated disciplines in some of the other sciences. The prime example at the time of this writing may be in the case of molecular biology, a relatively recent amalgam of earlier and disparate fields, a combination that may one day recombine with a current behavioral science to produce a yet unimagined new hybrid discipline.

What the behavioral sciences have in common is their concern, of course, with behavior—human and animal. However, not everyone who professes an interest in behavior is necessarily a behavioral scientist. Painters, novelists, and theologians are also concerned with behavior. But although they may have much of consequence to suggest to the behavioral scientist, still they themselves are not behavioral scientists. Nor, ordinarily, would they wish to be considered as such.

Although it is not easy to say just how the behavioral scientist's interest in behavior differs from anyone else's, in general, it is possible to differentiate the work of the professional student of behavior from that of others who share his interests. The work, or method, of the behavioral scientist is characterized by the systematic nature of his observations of behavior. The word systematic does not mean that there is *a* system for the observation of behavior but that there is a variety of methods of observation, each having evolved a set of formal and informal rules by which to assess its own adequacy. These rules have developed as a result of experience into a loose conception of what constitutes good scientific practice, and we consider examples of systematic observation in Chapter 2. That is, because a substantial segment of the behavioral science community feels that such practices "work" or "produce" or "pay off," they have come to be regarded as "good" scientific practices.

Good behavioral science is more, however, than just an exercise in systematic observation. Whether a program of research will "pay off" by casting new light on some difficult problem or by illuminating a perplexing aspect of behavior must also depend on the quality of the scientist's research ideas, or hypotheses. Where do research ideas come from? Constructing hypotheses in the behavioral sciences, like speculating on the meaning or basis of any puzzling issue, can be a varied and imaginative process. The method of logic in both cases is essentially the same, and it is the combination of logical discovery and systematic observation that can yield highly significant and reliable insights.

THE DEVELOPMENT OF HYPOTHESES

Suppose that we were interviewing someone for a position. We talk to him, observe his behavior, and think about his answers to our questions and his own questions. How would we form an impression of him? If we began by examining his resume—reading about his job experiences, education, hobbies, and interests—this background information might lead us to speculate on his abilities and limitations for the position. Or suppose something unexpected happened—a fire alarm, a spilled cup of coffee, an embarrassing slip of the tongue. His response might suddenly reveal a whole new side to his personality. Alternatively, we might detect a subtle inconsistency in something he said and hypothesize an additional attribute in order to reconcile the discrepant bit of information with our highly positive initial impression of him.

The structure of scientific discovery is no less logical than would be the deductions involved in our development of hypotheses about this job applicant. Just as hypotheses about his aptitudes emerge naturally with each increment of significant new data because we are perceptive interviewers, so will ideas develop for the perceptive scientist as new bits of evidence come into the picture. Not all ideas will be correct, although logic and scientific method will provide a means of ascertaining their probable correctness. Peter Caws has compared the structure of scientific discovery to the game of chess:

> . . . chess is, after all, a strictly deductive game, and all it takes to win every time is the ability to do a few billion calculations in the head within the period legally allowed for a move. Imagine a chess game in which there are some concealed pieces, moved by a third player, which influence the possible moves of the pieces on the board, and imagine that, instead of 16 pieces to a side, there are several million, some governed by rules of play not yet known to the players. In such a game a man who, after a long apprenticeship with the masters of his time, made three or four good moves during his career would have gained a place in history.
>
> The kind of inference a great scientist employs in his creative moments is comparable to the kind of inference the master at chess employs; it involves an ability to keep a lot of variables in mind at once, to be sensitive to feedback from tentative calculations (or experiments), to assess strategies for the deployment of time and resources, to perceive the relevance of one fact to another, or of a hypothesis to facts. The difference between his logic and our logic is one of degree, not of kind; we employ precisely the same methods, but more clumsily and on more homely tasks [Caws, 1969, p. 1379].

The structure of scientific discovery is thus seen as a natural deductive process. What perhaps separates the scientific genius from the rest of us is his ability to generate bold hypotheses without letting inhibiting factors intervene. But scientists are also human and as vulnerable to constraints on their creativity as anyone else. Indeed, there are a host of counterelements—substantive preconceptions, methodological biases, professional mores—that can inhibit the creative process by placing blinders on even the brightest, most perceptive individual. Barber (1961) mentioned the case of the scientist who, because he believed that cartilage was a relatively inert and uninteresting type of tissue, discounted his observation of floppiness in rabbits' ears after injecting the enzyme papain and so was blinded from making a discovery that eventually altered the established scientific view.

How are scientific hypotheses created in the first place? McGuire (1973) identified nine ways: the case study, the paradoxical incident, analogy, the hypothetico-deductive method, functional analysis, rules of thumb, conflicting results, accounting for exceptions, and straightening out complex relationships. The distinctions between categories are not always sharp—a given project can involve more than one creative approach—although it will be instructive to consider some examples of each, keeping in mind that these are just some of the routes to creative discovery in the behavioral sciences.

The Case Study

Exemplifying this first approach was a descriptive research project conducted by Allport, Bruner, and Jandorf (1953) that involved an analysis of over 200 autobiographies on the subject of "My life in Germany before and after January 30, 1933." Of this collection of case studies, 90 were subjected to a particularly searching psychological analysis. Most of the autobiographers were male, Jewish or Protestant, aged 30-60, middle class or upper class, and either from Germany or Austria. A striking finding was that despite the increasing probability of potential persecution, the evidence was minimized or denied—the truth may have been too hard for them to accept. By and large the histories were preconcentration camp reports, and no one yet knew what was to come. Still, there were severe stresses reported, including physical assaults, but even these were first seen by their victims as isolated and nonrepresentative events. Another finding characteristic of the 90 was that despite the stresses to which they had been exposed, there were no radical transformations in their personalities. People changed, to be sure, but they were still clearly identifiable as the same people.

All the respondents in the sample of 90 had experienced severe frustration, and there was an important theory—the frustration-aggression theory—that had just been formulated, which predicted that aggression and its derivatives should be the reaction to all frustration

(Dollard, Doob, Miller, Mowrer, & Sears, 1939). Case studies of these 90 lives, however, showed that there were many other reactions to frustration besides aggression and its offshoots. There were also responses of defeat, resignation, fantasy, conformity, and perhaps, above all, responses of planning and problem solving.

A similar type of study, but one that took over where the Allport, Bruner, and Jandorf study left off, was conducted by Boder (1949). After Germany's surrender in World War II, General Dwight D. Eisenhower sent out a call to the American press that can best be summarized by the phrase "Come and see for yourself." The dead of Auschwitz, Bergen-Belsen, Buchenwald, Dachau, and Treblinka outnumbered their survivors, but there *were* survivors, and Boder, who spoke Russian, German, Spanish, Yiddish, and English, set out to collect first-person statements of what had happened and how they had responded. The wire recorder had just been developed and made available commercially, so Boder was able to collect a verbatim statement from each of the concentration camp victims that he interviewed. The stimulus question for each respondent was "We know very little in America about the things that happened to you people who were in concentration camps. If you want to help us out . . . tell us . . . your name, how old you are, and where you were and what happened to you when the war started." Altogether, 70 people, selected for representativeness, were interviewed for a total of 120 hours. There was, of course, no guarantee of representativeness of these respondents, but the bias was likely to be in the direction of less horror for these survivors than for the typical resident of a concentration camp. As Boder's title stated: "He did not interview the dead."

In a sense, the case-study narratives collected by Boder were temporal continuations of those collected by Allport, Bruner, and Jandorf. Narratives collected by the latter went only up to the beginning of the war while the bulk of Boder's narratives were concerned only with the war years. The earlier investigators could hardly have imagined that the next half-dozen years would bring such a deluge of horrors. In order for Boder to be better able to understand the behavior of concentration camp victims, it was necessary for him to develop some system of classification of the stresses in the inmates' life situation. From this came the Traumatic Index, an indicator that permitted the classification of the common trauma reported by many of the survivors: confiscation of personal belongings and property; loadings onto cattle cars without food, water, or ventilation so that most "passengers" were dead before they arrived at their destination; the sortings into groups of those strong enough still to be able to do forced labor versus those too sick or weak or young to work and, therefore, directly taken to the "showers" that produced not water but poison gas; the loading of bodies onto the crematorium piles when one could not be sure the gas had done its work.

The case-study approach lends itself to all sorts of interesting variations in addition to the use of autobiographical data. Cultural anthropologists make intensive case analyses of small groups and societies, sometimes by observing participants from a distance and other times by actually engaging in the host culture as a participant-observer. Thus, Paine (1970) studied information management among the nomadic reindeer owners of Kautokeino, discovering that gossip was used as a tool for settling questions of authority in connection with herd management and other daily problems among the Lapland pastoralists. In another study of gossiping, this one in a Polynesian society, Firth (1956) discovered that hearsay was not just a product of idle curiosity or fantasy but served as a societal restraint to help the group gain purposive ends.

The Paradoxical Incident

Latané and Darley's (1970) development of the diffusion-of-responsibility hypothesis is a good example of this second approach to scientific discovery. The paradoxical incident that inspired their inquiry was a famous murder that occurred in a respectable Queens neighborhood in New York City. Kitty Genovese, coming home at 3 o'clock in the morning, was set upon by a maniac who stabbed her repeatedly. Although her cries of terror were heard by at least three dozen residents, not one person went to her aid, and she died before anyone even bothered to call the police (Rosenthal, 1964). To account for this frightening passivity, Latané and Darley postulated that social responsibility may be dissipated when more people are present during an emergency. Through a series of experiments, they soon developed the hypothesis further to describe a steplike series of responses made by people called upon to lend their assistance in a crisis. The first step is noticing that an emergency is occurring. Because it is usually considered in bad taste for Americans to look too closely at people in public, this cultural disposition may work to inhibit prosocial behavior. The second step is deciding that the occurrence is actually an emergency. Even if one gets past the first stage of noticing that someone is lying on the sidewalk, one still has to decide whether the person is asleep or drunk or if he is sick or has been mugged. The third step is to make a personal commitment to intervene. When Kitty Genovese was attacked, 38 people witnessed her plight, and each decided that something was wrong but not one person made a move to intervene.

To test their diffusion-of-responsibility hypothesis, Latané and Darley conducted a wide variety of laboratory and field experiments where critical variables in the situation could be manipulated. In one study, students at Columbia University who had volunteered to be in a discussion of problems in urban college living, noticed a stream of smoke beginning to puff into their room through a wall vent. If one other student was in the room there was a much greater chance of his reporting the difficulty than if there were three or more present. Instead of reporting the emergency when students were together in a group, the diffusion-of-responsibility phenomenon appeared to take over, and they became passive and dismissed their apprehensions through rationalization.

There are other examples of a paradoxical incident inspiring a scientific insight. In trying to account for the paradox that earthquake victims gossiped about future catastrophes instead of seeking gratification in fantasy, Leon Festinger (1957) was inspired, in large part, to postulate his famous theory of cognitive dissonance. Rumors about the future, he hypothesized, may be attempts to reduce cognitive dissonance by providing a future justification for unfounded anxieties.

Analogy

McGuire's (1964) inoculation theory provides an impressive example of the use of analogy in the generation of scientific hypotheses. Early in his thinking, he was inspired by a series of studies by Janis, Lumsdaine, and Gladstone (1951) and Lumsdaine and Janis (1953) that showed that the effect of having been exposed to preliminary propaganda was to reduce the impact of subsequent counterpropaganda. Proceeding from this finding, McGuire designed a program of research to test an attitude inoculation model patterned on the biological analogy. In order to immunize someone against counterpropaganda, perhaps it is advisable to expose him to some of the counterarguments and let him build up his defenses, just as being exposed to a live virus will help to build up the body's defenses by stimulating the production of antibodies. Of course, being exposed to too many counterarguments, like too heavy a dose of the live virus, could have the opposite effect: reducing resistance rather than strengthening it. If the analogy is correct, the problem is to establish the safe amount of counterargumentation in an inoculation that would help build a defense to ward off a massive attack by the same counterpropaganda in the future, without changing the subject's attitudes in the direction of the counterpropaganda in the process.

McGuire's idea was that cultural truisms (e.g., "Cigarette smoking is bad for your health"), because they exist in a kind of "germ-free" environment where their validity is never challenged, should be especially vulnerable to counterarguments. The analogy was compared to the biological situation in which a person brought up in a germ-free environment will be highly vulnerable to diseases because his body, never having been exposed to weakened doses of viruses, has not built up an immunity to diseases. Using various forms of prior defenses to test the theory, McGuire was able to establish some optimum procedures for inoculating people against propaganda counter to their beliefs in cultural truisms.

Another example of this approach was in Milgram's (1970) theoretical work using a computer systems analogy and the concept of stimulus overload to explain the sensation and repercussions of overcrowding. The sensation is most keenly felt in places like midtown Manhattan, where it has been estimated that as many as a quarter of a million people may be encountered by the average worker within a 10-minute walk from his office. Milgram hypothesized that the psychological link to understanding how city dwellers have adapted to this phenomenon is provided by the concept of overload, a term drawn from systems analysis where new inputs cannot be adequately processed because the machine already has too many old or ongoing inputs with which to cope. He hypothesized six alternative adaptive responses to overload, roughly consistent with the computer analogy. (1) A person may choose to disregard less personally important inputs—for example, ignoring the sick drunk who is lying on the pavement. (2) He may allow less time to each input—spending less time with the family because of the pressures and demands of work. (3) Inputs may be shifted by redrawing the boundaries of responsibility—requiring bus passengers to have the exact change. (4) Stimuli can be blocked off before they have a chance to enter the system—the unlisted telephone number. (5) Substitute devices can be used to absorb inputs—public welfare programs to handle the needy. (6) Very strong inputs can be filtered out altogether as in the case of censorship.

The Hypothetico-Deductive Method

This approach splices together plausible principles and then teases out predictions from their conjunction. For example, in their study of the primacy-recency question, Miller and Campbell (1959) used the hypothetico-deductive method of constructing hypotheses.

When attitudes are influenced more by arguments presented first, this is called primacy. When they are influenced more by arguments presented last, the effect is termed recency. The scientific question concerns the conditions under which either effect will be favored. If you were in a debate, would it be to your advantage to speak first, or last? Which has the advantage in the courtroom by virtue of the prescribed order of presentation of arguments, the prosecution or the defense? To generate hypotheses on the problem, Miller and Campbell combined the so-called "Ebbinghaus curves for forgetting" with a principle known as Jost's law to deduce some conditions favoring primacy and recency. According to the Ebbinghaus curves, we tend to forget information in a neat, systematic way that can be described by a gradually downward sloping line. If, after a two-hour lecture, you did not make a special effort to remember the information, normally you should forget almost half of what you heard shortly after the lecture was completed. After a little while longer, the amount of forgetting would level off. Research had shown that there was at least some slight advantage in presenting one's arguments first, and Miller and Campbell thus postulated that, given the applicability of the Ebbinghaus curves, the strength of the curve for initial information would have to start a little higher to reflect this advantage. Figure 1 shows this reasoning in the slightly higher peak for the curve associated with message A. An example of A and B could be a political debate where both sides were presented one after the other. An example of A and B' could be a weekly televised series of speeches where speaker A was presented first and speaker B' a week later. Bringing Jost's law into the picture—when two associations are equally strong at the moment, the older association will decay less rapidly than the newer—one can see how Miller and Campbell deduced predictions of primacy and recency by considering the element of timing in speeches and measurements.

Functional Analysis

Explaining how people function is a fifth approach to the structure of discovery in the behavioral sciences, and it has stimulated the development of several functional analyses of rumormongering.

Allport and Postman (1947), proceeding on the Gestalt assertion that processes distribute themselves to produce maximum order and simplicity, constructed a theory that postulated that rumors will emerge whenever events are important and news is lacking or ambiguous. The principal motivational force in rumormongering, they reasoned, is the pursuit of meaning and good closure. Because our minds protest against chaos and we seek to extract meaning from our environment, there must be an intellectual pressure to pursue good closure, which may account for the vitality of many rumors. The psychoanalyst Carl G. Jung (1910, 1959) proposed an entirely different view of rumormonger-

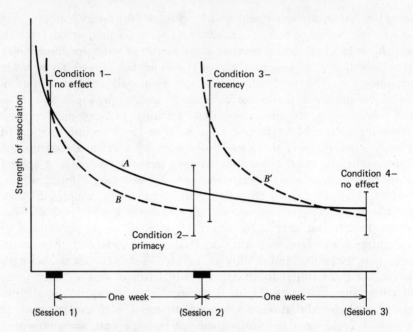

FIGURE 1. Hypothetical curves showing the rate of forgetting for message *A* (solid line) and opposing message *B* or *B'* (dashed lines.) The slight initial advantage for the first position is shown by the higher strength of association for message *A*, which was introduced first. *B* symbolizes an opposing message presented immediately after *A* was concluded, and *B'* symbolizes an opposing message presented after a week's delay. If a measurement were taken just after *A* and *B* had occurred (condition 1), or if it were taken one week after *A* and *B'* (condition 4), there should be no advantage for primacy or recency as the gradients would be at about the same level of association strength. If a measurement were taken one week after *A* and *B* had occurred (condition 2), primacy should be favored because the solid line (for message *A*) is higher in association strength than the dashed line (for message *B*). If a measurement were taken immediately after *A* and *B'* had occurred (condition 3), recency should be favored as the gradient for message *B'* would have a higher association strength. (After Miller and Campbell, 1959.)

ing based on his notion that it gives vent to anxieties and hostilities. The socioanthropological view, alluded to earlier, argues that rumors function as collective, problem-solving transactions. In the work of Shibutani (1966), for example, the idea is that societies, being in a state of flux, give rise to crises whenever new events are inexplicable in terms of established assumptions. For people to act in concert, they must alter their orientations to these new events together. By consulting with each other and comparing each other's impressions—rumor being an integral part of the process—they develop new ways of coping with their ever-changing world.

The well-constructed theory is one whose assumptions can also be put to an empirical test, and, at least in the case of Allport and Postman's formulation, this criterion has been met. For example, Schachter and Burdick (1955) tested the proposition that rumormongering will increase when there is widespread cognitive unclarity. In this study, which took place in a small, exclusive girls' preparatory school, the principal interrupted work in several classes, pointed a finger at one girl and announced, "Miss K_____, would you get your hat, coat and books, please, and come with me. You will be gone for the rest of the day." This unprecedented incident, which was intended to produce a situation of cognitive unclarity for the rest of the class, was preceded a day or two before by the planting, unobtrusively, of a rumor that some exams were missing. Consistent with the theory, twice as many exchanges of information occurred in the classes in which the girl had been removed than in those where the exam rumor had been planted but no one was removed.

Rules of Thumb

In this case one observes the practitioner's rule of thumb and, assuming that it must work, tries to duplicate and explain the phenomenon. Dabbs and Janis (1965) and Janis, Kaye, and Kirschner (1965) employed this device in studying the technique used by salesmen for softening up their clients by discussing business over a good lunch. Their laboratory test of the phenomenon consisted of feeding hungry Yale undergraduates soda pop and peanuts at the same time the students read propaganda messages, and then comparing the effects with those in an unfed control group. Repeating the sort of "things-go-better-with-Coke effect" so familiar to the professional salesman, they discovered that there was a momentary mood of compliance operating in the fed group that made them more susceptible to the propaganda than in the comparison group that read the propaganda but got nothing to eat.

A similar approach has guided other research in social psychology. Freedman and Fraser (1966) studied the foot-in-the-door technique whereby an agreement to a small request is followed by compliance with a larger request. In two field experiments where subjects were initially asked to do such things as lend their name to a petition and then, in the larger request, install on their front lawn a sign relevant to the petition, the investigators found empirical support for the old adage, "If you give them an inch, they'll take a mile."

Doob, Carlsmith, Freedman, Landauer, and Tom (1969) also studied a sequential rule of thumb although their findings were diametrically opposite to the principle drawn from intuition, which guides marketers who use the familiar "introductory low-price offer" gambit. Typically, a new product is offered at a low price, and then the price is increased when buyer resistance is supposedly overcome. To test this idea these investigators used matched pairs of discount houses that sold the same product at either a discounted price or the regular price for a short period of time. However, when the prices were eventually equated in all the stores, the sales were higher where the initial price had been high. In this case, then, the researchers' finding tended to refute the rule-of-thumb hypohesis.

Conflicting Results

A seventh approach is in trying to account for conflicting observations. In a sense, the Miller and Campbell study, discussed in connection with the hypothetico-deductive method, also illustrates this way of generating hypotheses, since it offered a paradigm for predicting the occurrence of quite opposite effects: primacy and recency. Other behavioral scientists who have been inspired to adopt this approach include Zajonc (1965), in his theoretical development of the social facilitation hypothesis, and Goldstein and Arms (1971), in their Army-Navy football game study on the effects of witnessing an aggressive sport.

Zajonc neatly integrated a body of seemingly conflicting results regarding the psychological effect of the presence of other people by hypothesizing that, in general, the presence of others impairs the learning of new tasks but facilitates the performance of well-learned ones. The studies he summarized were done on such diverse populations as cockroaches, ants, rats, college undergraduates, and Army reservists. Some studies showed that behavior improved when observers were present, and some showed it becoming poorer in the presence of others. To reconcile these conflicting results, Zajonc based his explanation on the familiar finding in psychology that a high-drive level will cause people to give the dominant response to a stimulus. When the task is familiar and well learned, the dominant response should be the correct one; when the task is new or not well learned, the dominant response could just as well be the incorrect as the correct one. Reasoning that the presence of others must serve to increase the subject's drive level, and that this increase in drive is what leads to dominant responses, Zajonc concluded that the presence of others must inhibit the learning of new responses and facilitate the performance of well-learned ones. Other things being equal, from the social facilitation principle a student might be advised to study alone, preferably in an isolated cubicle, and, once the material is well learned, to take the examination with as many other students as possible, preferably on a stage before a large audience.

The work of Goldstein and Arms took a quite different quasi-experimental tack. According to several theorists, including Sigmund Freud, witnessing violent behavior in others should serve to reduce the aggressiveness of the observer by draining him of his hostilities. Some have even suggested that international conflicts might be reduced by staging massive competitive sporting events between nations, which presumably would serve as emotional catharses for the audiences. The opposing view contends that watching violence will arouse hostilities and aggressiveness in the observers. Here, the idea is that the observer tends to imitate the violence he has witnessed, particularly if he has seen it rewarded. Goldstein and Arms pitted these conflicting observations against each other in a study that assessed hostility among observers at an Army-Navy football game. They found that it made no difference whether the spectators' preferred team won or lost the game; observers were significantly more hostile after witnessing the contest than before. When the study was repeated during an intercollegiate gymnastics meet, a nonaggressive sport, there was no change in hostility.

The Goldstein and Arms study also illustrates a special case of scientific thinking, which Platt (1964) has called strong inference. By pitting alternative views against each other in a specially devised study, one of the hypotheses may be ruled out. However, there is a danger in the procedure. When strongly divergent points of view are advocated based on quite different observations of the same situation by competent observers, it may be true that both viewpoints are correct. The hypothesis that was ruled out by the data might only be "incorrect" under the given set of conditions in which it was tested in that particular strong-inference study. An example of the dilemma can be seen in the case of the so-called adding versus averaging controversy in social psychology (cf. Rosnow, 1972; Rosnow and Arms, 1968; Rosnow, Wainer, and Arms, 1970).

The clustering process, by which the mind consolidates related ideas and perceptions into distinct categories, is an important agent of attitude formation. While we are not sure exactly how it works, some recent studies suggest that the clustering process tends to conform to certain predictive mathematical rules. Investigators in the area of impression formation have observed two recurrent patterns of clustering from which they have drawn two alternative rules. These are the adding principle and the averaging principle. The first states that perceptions combine in a manner corresponding roughly to a mathematical summing formula; the second, that an averaging formula more accurately predicts the manner in which perceptions will cluster. To illustrate, suppose that two persons, *A* and *B*, each make $50 a day and that a third person, *C*, makes $40 a day. Which group enjoys higher economic status, a group consisting of *A* and *B* or a group consisting of all three? Normally we would use the averaging principle and say that *A* and *B* is a wealthier group than *A*, *B*, and *C*. But now imagine that *A*, *B*, and *C* are members of the same family. In this case, we would probably use the adding formula and say that *A*, *B*, and *C* is the wealthier group.

Thus, clustering will conform to whichever rule the mind invokes, and a strong inference experiment that ruled out either principle could be premature in its conclusions. Adding our observations on the characteristics of an ethnic group yields a stereotype that circumscribes all extremes. Averaging our observations yields a stereotype that makes greater allowances for individual differences. In practice we do some of both.

Accounting for Exceptions

The discovery of the sleeper effect is a good illustration of this eighth approach to hypothesis construction. In a program of communications research conducted by Hovland, Lumsdaine, and Sheffield (1949) during World War II, it was suspected that the advantage of having a prestigious communicator endorse an opinion might tend to diminish over time. Prestige suggestion was a cardinal rule among specialists in the mass media, and the sleeper effect seemed to be an important exception. If an opinion were attributed to a very respected source, as opposed to being associated with an un-admired source, the initial advantage would, of course, usually favor the positive communicator. Over a period of time, however, the difference in persuasiveness between the two communicators may dissipate, leaving neither with an advantage.

Several years after the war, this delayed effect in influenceability —the sleeper effect—was demonstrated by Hovland and Weiss (1951; cf. Gillig and Greenwald, 1974). During a lecture in an advanced college history class, they exposed the students to arguments on several controversial issues. Choosing a class, and one other than in psychology, was a way to coordinate the materials into a regular pattern of lectures without arousing the subjects' suspicions too much. In half the cases the arguments were attributed to a very prestigious source, and for the remaining subjects the arguments were attributed to a source who was perceived as untrustworthy. As anticipated from the rule of prestige suggestion, more initial agreement with an argument occurred among those subjects who were exposed to the material attributed to the respected source. However, one month later, when the subjects' opinions were measured again, the net effect was to cancel the initial advantage of prestige suggestion. With the passage of time the students tended to separate the content of the message from its sources, and so the originally untrustworthy source material became more acceptable.

Straightening Out Complex Relationships

Still another way of developing hypotheses in the behavioral sciences involves reducing complex relationships to a simpler, more parsimonious theoretical structure. Various examples already given also exemplify this ninth approach. Festinger's cognitive dissonance theory reduced what appeared to be some complicated, counterintuitive relationships to a more comprehensible formulation. Milgram's explanation of the urban experience, Miller and Campbell's primacy-recency model, and Shibutani's work on rumormongering all illustrate the approach as well.

The sociologist Erving Goffman has shown how complex behaviors can be understood in simpler terms. He has interpreted face-to-face interactions in natural settings as ritual, using the concept of "face-work" as a device for clarifying this complicated behavior (Goffman, 1955). He has done similar analyses of the nature of deference and demeanor, embarrassment, alienation from interaction, and psychologically maladaptive behaviors, in each case straightening out otherwise complex, almost unintelligible, relationships in verbal and nonverbal social interactions (Goffman, 1956a, 1956b, 1957).

Social psychologist Uriel G. Foa (1971) has performed a similar function in his development of a theory of resource exchange to straighten out the complex relationships involved in interpersonal behavior. Viewing such behavior as an exchange of resources characterized by profits and losses, he demonstrated a definite structural pattern in the interrelationship of resources. In Foa's view, there are six classes of resources —information, status, love, services, goods, and money—that he plotted on a two-coordinate space according to their particularism (the significance of the person providing the resource) and concreteness (whether it is symbolic or conceptually concrete). To illustrate, love—because awareness of its source is always a highly significant factor—anchors the high end of the particularism dimension, whereas money, for just the opposite reason, falls at the low end. Status and services are seen to be conceptually closer to love, and information and goods are closer to money. Should there be a deficit in one of these resources, there will be an effort to compensate for, or recoup, the loss. Thus, love may be bartered for status or money, money for goods or services, and so on. Foa's research has shown that proximal resources tend to be perceived as similar, that people will tend to reciprocate using resources similar to those from which they have benefited, and that they prefer to retaliate in kind when they have suffered a loss (Foa and Foa, 1974). By reducing complex interpersonal behavior to a more simple, parsimonious level of comprehension, Foa's discovery offers a sharper insight into problems of modern society. For example, recasting what is known on the problem of rumormongering in this theoretical mold may provide a more general, integrative conceptualization and also lead to new hypotheses with regard to its specific functions (cf. Rosnow, 1974).

SERENDIPITY IN SCIENCE

While these various examples of the structure of discovery in the behavioral sciences all show an orderly chain of detectivelike inquiry coupled with perspicacity and natural deduction, sometimes great scientific discoveries are made purely by accident. Merton (1968) has discussed this fascinating phenomenon of discovery by chance—called the pattern of serendipity—in sociological inquiry, and there have been many instances of such unanticipated, anomalous discoveries outside the behavioral sciences as well. The essence of the serendipity pattern is that some unexpected data exert pressure upon the investigator for a new direction of inquiry.

Lovell (1972), for example, has mentioned the recent case of Professor Hewish of Cambridge University who was observing the scintillation —the variations in strength—of radio signals from distant objects in the universe. One of the professor's young research students, Jocelyn Bell, noticed on several occasions that there were scintillations occurring near midnight, when the normal interplanetary pattern is generally absent. After months of exploration, Hewish finally concluded that the phenomenon was being caused by a pulsating signal of extraterrestrial origin. The new data prompted a whole new direction of investigation, so that now it can be hypothesized that these pulsating radio sources, or pulsars, may be rapidly spinning neutron stars that would have resulted from the collapse of stars in supernova explosions. It is a wise researcher who, while on the trail of some logically deduced expectation, also keeps a watchful eye out for the unanticipated, anomalous discovery.

chapter two

systematic observation

ORIENTATIONS

We began by characterizing the method of the behavioral scientist in terms of the systematic nature of his observations. It is possible to distinguish two principal types of systematic observation, the descriptive and the relational, and a special case of the second type, called experimental observation. Once the research problem has been identified, it is important to select the orientation that is most appropriate to the situation.

Descriptively oriented observation tends to have as its goal a careful mapping out of what happens behaviorally. The researcher who is interested in the study of children's failure in school may spend a good deal of time observing the classroom behavior of children who are doing poorly; he can then describe as carefully as possible what it was he observed. Careful observation of failing pupils might lead to some revision of our concepts of classroom failure, to suggestions as to factors that may have contributed to the development of failure, and even perhaps to ideas for the remediation of failure.

The careful observation of behavior may be a necessary first step in the development of a program of research in the behavioral sciences, but it is rarely regarded as sufficient. Sooner or later someone will want to know *why* something happens behaviorally or *how* what happens behaviorally is related to other events. If our interest is in children's failure, we are not likely to be satisfied for very long with even the

17

most careful description of that behavior. Sooner or later we will want to know the antecedents of failure and the outcomes of various proceures designed to reduce classroom failure. Even if we were not motivated directly by the practical implications of knowing the causes and cures of failure, we would believe our understanding of it to be considerably improved if we knew the conditions increasing and decreasing its likelihood. To learn about the increase or decrease of failure behavior, or any other behavior, observations must focus on at least two elements at the same time—two sets of observations must be made that can be related to one another.

Relationally oriented observation has as its goal the description of how what happens behaviorally changes along with changes in some other set of observations. Continuing with the classroom example, let us suppose that the researcher noted that many of the scholastically failing subjects were rarely looked at or addressed by their teachers and seldom exposed to new academically relevant information by the teachers. At this stage he might have only an impression about the relation between pupils' learning failures and teachers' teaching behavior. Such impressions of relationships are a frequent, and a frequently valuable, by-product of descriptive observation. But, if they are to be taken seriously as systematic relational observations, they cannot be left at the impressionistic level for very long. Our observer, or perhaps another observer who wanted to see for himself if the first observer's impressions were accurate, might arrange to make a series of coordinate observations on a sample of pupils in classrooms that adequately represented the population of pupils about whom some conclusion was to be drawn. For each pupil it could be noted (a) whether he was learning anything or the degree to which he had been learning and (b) the degree to which his teacher had been exposing him to material to be learned. From such coordinate observations, it should be possible to make a quantitative statement of the relationship between pupils' exposure to material to be learned and the amount of such material that they did in fact learn.

To carry the illustration one step further, suppose that pupils exposed to less information were also those who tended to learn less. On discovering this relationship there might be a temptation to suggest that children learn less because they are taught less. Such a suggestion, while plausible, would not be warranted by the relationship reported. It might be the case, for example, that teachers teach less to those they already know to be less able to learn. Differences in teacher teaching behavior, then, may be as much a result of their pupil's learning as a determinant of that learning. If we wanted to pursue our hypothesis, we could arrange to make further systematic relational observations that would allow us to infer whether differences in information presented to pupils, apart from any individual differences among them, affected the pupils' learning. Such questions are best answered by a very important type of relational observation that involves the observer's specifically manipulating the conditions he believes to be responsible for some effect. These specially arranged relational observations are termed experimental observations.

Experimental observation, a special case of relational observation, has as its goal the description of what happens behaviorally when something of interest to the experimenter is introduced into the situation. Experimental observation is especially powerful in that it permits answers to questions of the form: "What leads to what?" Nonexeprimental relational observations can only rarely provide such information and then only under very special conditions. The increase in power in going from nonexperimental to experimental observations is the increase in power in going from statements of "X is related to Y" to statements of "X is responsible for Y." In our example, teacher teaching is X and pupil learning is Y. Our experiment is designed to reveal the effects of teacher teaching on pupil learning. We might, therefore, select a sample of youngsters and, by tossing a fair coin or by some other random method, divide them into two equivalent groups. One of these groups would have more information given them by their teachers, while the other group would be given less information. We could then assess which group of children showed the superior learning. If the two groups differed, we would be in a position to ascribe the difference to the different treatments we had applied: more, compared to less, information.

There might still be a question of what it was about the better procedure that led to the improvement. In the case of increased teacher teaching, for example, we might wonder whether it was the information itself, the increased attention from the teacher as she presented the additional material, any concomitant increases in eye contact, smiles, warmth, or other possible correlates of increased teaching behavior. Each of these more-refined hypotheses about the effective agents or active ingredients could itself be investigated in further studies involving descriptive and/or relational observations of the experimental or non-experimental kinds. (Incidentally, for the teaching situation we have been using as an example, it turns out that the amount of new material teachers expose to their pupils is sometimes predictable, not so much by the children's actual learning ability, but by their teachers' beliefs or expectations for the pupils' learning ability—Beez, 1968; Rosenthal, 1973b. The basic idea that teachers' expectations about pupils' performance can come to serve as self-fulfilling prophecies was investi-

Table 1. Sample Statements Based on Descriptive Observation

Investigators	Statement
DeVore and Hall (1965)	Baboon groups vary in size from 9 to 185.
Milgram (1963)	A majority of research subjects were willing to administer an allegedly dangerous level of electric shock to another person as long as they were requested to do so by a person in authority.
Matarazzo, Wiens, and Saslow (1965)	When people are being interviewed for Civil Service positions, the length of their utterances tends to be a mirror image of the letter J. That is to say, most utterances are quite short in duration with only a few lasting as long as a full minute.

gated experimentally by Rosenthal and Jacobson, 1968, and subsequent work is summarized briefly by Rosenthal, 1973c.)

The types of conclusions or inferences drawn on the basis of these three types of observation are thus quite different. Table 1 shows that statements based on descriptive observation tell "how things are." Table 2 shows that statements based on nonexperimental relational observation also tell "how things are" but, more specifically, how they are in relation to other things. Table 3 shows that statements based on experimental relational observation tell "how things are" but also tell one or more of the ways things can get to be that way.

If you review some of the various examples of hypothesis construction given in Chapter 1, you will find many applications of these three orientations from different areas in the behavioral sciences. Returning to the first two examples, the personal documents studied by Allport, Bruner, and Jandorf, and later by Boder, were employed in a generally descriptive manner. There was also perhaps an implied relational intent in both studies. Looking only at the samples examined, the data would be called descriptive; but if we emphasize that both studies were interested in learning more about behavior under conditions of catastrophe, we might also view the intent as relational. By implication at least, the question could be viewed as "What is the effect of people's being exposed to catastrophic situations compared to their not being exposed to such situations?" However, it will also be instructive to consider some detailed examples of each type of orientation all from the same research area, and the field of personality offers an excellent case in point.

Table 2. Sample Statements Based on Relational Observation

Investigators	Statement
DeVore and Hall (1965)	Baboon groups found at higher elevations tend to have fewer members.
Milgram (1965)	Research subjects who are more willing to administer electric shocks to other persons report themselves as somewhat more tense during their research participation than do subjects who are less willing to apply electric shocks to others.
Matarazzo, Wiens, and Saslow (1965)	In interviewing both normal subjects as well as mental patients, it was found that average speech durations were longest with normals and shortest with the most disturbed patients.

Table 3. Sample Statements Based on Experimental Observation

Investigators	Statement
Harlow (1959)	Rhesus monkey infants prefer cloth-covered inanimate mother-surrogates to wire mesh type mother-surrogates.
Milgram (1965)	Research subjects are less obedient to orders to administer electric shocks to other persons when they are in close rather than remote contact with these persons.
Matarazzo, Wiens, and Saslow (1965)	In interviewing applicants for Civil Service positions, the length of the applicants' utterances could be approximately doubled simply by the interviewer's approximately doubling the length of his utterances.

DESCRIPTIVE RESEARCH

Scientific inquiry in personality psychology runs the full gamut of types of research. Perhaps more so than is the case for most areas of psychology, personality research has been characterized by an emphasis on the descriptive level of observation. With all the excellent descriptive level research available, one program stands out as perhaps the paradigmatic case of descriptive observation in the field of personality. This was the program of assessment carried out by the OSS Assessment Staff (1948).

The Office of Strategic Services was a World War II government agency charged with tasks as varied as intelligence gathering, sabotage behind enemy lines, mobilization of guerilla groups to resist the Nazi occupation, and the preparation and dissemination of propaganda. Thousands of men, drawn from both military and civilian life, were recruited to carry out the often hazardous missions of the OSS, though initially it was not known what type of men to select for each of the various types of missions. Accordingly, a group of psychologists and psychiatrists was assembled to aid in the assessment of the special agents of the OSS. The chief contribution of these experts on personality was to set up a series of situations that would permit more useful and relevant descriptions of the personalities of the candidates. The original intent of the assessment group had been more ambitious. It had been hoped that it would be possible to lower appreciably the error rate in the selection of men and women for the OSS and to increase the likelihood of assignment of agents to those missions they could best perform. Unfortunately, from the point of view of this intent, several factors made impossible the development of a screening and placement system that could be fairly and properly evaluated. Chief among these factors were the assessment staff's not knowing what particular mission would be assigned to a recruit and, perhaps most importantly, several weaknesses in the final appraisal of how good a job an agent had actually done.

From December, 1943 to August, 1945, more than five thousand recruits were studied by the assessment staff at one or another station. The primary station, S, was located about an hour's ride from Washington, D. C., in a rustic setting of rolling meadows and stately trees. To this station, recruits were sent for a thrree-and-a-half-day period, during which they were given identical clothes to wear and carried a pseudonym so that colonels and privates and college professors would be indistinguishable to the assessment staff. Besides a false name, each recruit had to construct a cover story giving himself a new occupation, new residence, new place of birth, and a new educational background. Candidates were warned that the assessment staff would try to trick them into breaking cover and giving away their true identity.

Virtually everything that a recruit did from the moment he arrived at Station *S* was grist for the assessment mill. How he got off the truck that brought his group of recruits, the manner in which he asked questions of the staff member who explained the Station *S* procedures to the candidates, what he said at the first dinner, and what he chose to do after dinner when he was free to read, or talk, or withdraw. That first evening, candidates filled out a great many different paper-and-pencil tests of personality and ability and personal background information.

The next few days were filled with many situational tests in which the staff would have the opportunity to see each man's level of initiative, leadership, functioning intelligence, social relationships, and physical ability. For example, in one situation a group of four to seven men had to move a log and a rock across an eight-foot-wide brook. The situation was rigged so that either a bridge or an overhead cable system could be constructed to solve the problem, but the achievement of a solution was not the main purpose of the exercise. Instead, it was to give the staff an opportunity to see which man played what role in the team effort required to achieve a solution.

One of the most trying, and possibly also most revealing, situations was another task in which the candidate was to direct the efforts of two helpers in building a five-foot cube out of a giant tinker-toy set. Ostensibly, the task was to assess the candidate's leadership ability. In actuality, it was a test of stress tolerance. The two helpers, as it turned out, were really two members of the assessment staff called "Kippy" and "Buster." Kippy was a passive sort who did nothing unless ordered to, except occasionally to get in the way. Buster offered useless suggestions, griped repeatedly, and excelled in finding and harping on the candidate's weaknesses. Kippy and Buster together were sufficiently obstructive that, in the history of the OSS assessment program, no recruit was ever able to complete the task in the allotted ten minutes.

Some of the candidates perceived immediately that the two helpers were members of the assessment staff, and this knowledge sometimes, but not always, helped the candidates to contain their temper and persist in trying to get the job done. Other candidates wondered why the OSS could not afford better farmhands around the estate and admitted that the obstreperousness and insolence of the helpers tempted them more than once to lay an uncharitable hand upon one or the other of them. On more than one occasion such a laying on of hands did, in fact, occur. Some candidates learned enough about themselves from this experience that they asked to be excused from the program, deciding that they could not deal with stress of this kind.

During the candidates' half-week assessment period, they underwent many situational tests of the kind described. Table 4 lists some

Table 4. Some Situational Tests Employed by the OSS Assessment Staff

Situation	Props and Materials	Objective
Personal belongings	A man's personal effects including clothing, news clippings, time tables, ticket receipt	Assess the type of person who left these personal belongings
The brook	Log, rock, boards, rope, pulley, barrel	Transport log and rock across an eight-foot brook
The wall	Two walls, ten feet high, eight feet apart, heavy log, old board, short 2x4s	Transport heavy log up first wall, over to second wall, down second wall
Construction task	Giant tinker toy	Direct two uncooperative assistants in building a five-foot cube
Intelligence interview	Escaped prisoner	Interrogate prisoner for strategic information
Captured spy	Secret files	Explain why he was found at night going through secret files in government building where he did not work
Poststress attempt to break cover	Sympathetic staff member cordially trying to break cover	Discuss the captured-spy stress interview
Captured document analysis	Four captured documents	Abstract the core of reliable intelligence contained
Mined road	Long logs, stones, rope, 2x4s	Lead a group across a mined road
Room search	Friendly agent's room	Search room and report its contents by radio despite arrival of German guard
Blown bridge	Bridge abutments, pilings and debris	Lead a group across a river using only the remains of the blown bridge

of these tests, each one providing an opportunity for the staff to observe and describe carefully the behavior of the candidate. It seems unlikely that, either before or since, have so many people been observed and described so carefully by so many experts in human behavior.

We have viewed the OSS assessment project as a paradigmatic case of descriptive observation, but it must be noted again that description had not been the only goal of the assessment staff. They had also had a hope of relational observations in which the assessments made of the candidates could later be correlated with how good a job the men did in the field. Such correlations define the validity of the selection procedures, and, when they are adequately high, they tell that the predictor variable, the assessment in this case, does its job of predicting the outcome (or criterion variable), the actual job performance. Unfortunately, this type of relational outcome research had not been planned from the beginning, so there was no satisfactory evaluation of just how good a job had been done by the agents in the field. Even if such criterion information had been available, however, there is reason to suspect that the assessment program could hardly have been very effective since the staff had only the vaguest, and probably sometimes erroneous, ideas of the nature of the specific jobs for which the candidates were actually being selected. It would be unreasonable indeed to think that one could select people for the performance of unspecified functions.

RELATIONAL RESEARCH

The OSS assessment staff had been in a position to make a great many detailed observations relevant to many of the candidate's motives. However, there was not a planned, systematic attempt to relate the scores or ratings on any one of these motives to the scores or ratings on some subsequently measured variable that, on the basis of theory, should show a strong correlation with the predictor variable. In the field of personality research there are, however, many studies that could serve well to illustrate relational research. There are hundreds of studies showing how one personality attribute is related to some other personality attribute. For our illustration, we will discuss the development of a personality construct in which a means for its measurement was devised and then related to subjects' performance in a variety of other spheres as the construct would predict. Even when we narrow the range of personality research to such enterprises, there is still much to choose from. There are, for example, the brilliant investigations of David Mc-Clelland (1961) on the achievement motive and Stanley Schachter (1959) on the affiliation motive. For our example we will focus on a somewhat more recent, but similarly outstanding, program of research on a different motive: the motive to be approved by others.

At the very end of the 1950s Douglas Crowne and David Marlowe, both then at Ohio State University, set out to develop an instrument that would measure the need for social approval independent of the subjects' level of psychopathology. They began by considering hundreds of personality test items that were answered in a true-false format. To be included, an item had to be one that would reflect socially approved behavior but yet be almost certain to be untrue. In short, the items had to reflect behavior too good to be true. In addition, answers to the items should not have any implications of psychological abnormality of psychopathology. By having a group of psychology graduate students and faculty judge the social desirability of each item and by having another group of psychology graduate students and faculty judge the degree of psychopathology implied by each item, it was possible to develop a set of items that would reflect behavior too virtuous to be probable and yet carrying no implication of personal maladjustment. The final form of the test, called the Marlowe-Crowne Social-Desirability Scale, included 33 items (Crowne and Marlowe, 1964).

In about half the items a "true" answer reflects the socially desirable or higher need for approval response, and in about half the items a "false" answer reflects the socially desirable response. An example of the former type item might be: "I have never intensely disliked anyone," while an example of the latter might be: "I sometimes feel resentful when I don't get my way."

The items, combined to form a personality scale, showed a high degree of relationship with those measures with which the scale was expected to show high correlations. First, it correlated well with itself; that is, an impressive relationship was obtained between the two testings of a group of subjects who were tested one month apart. Thus, the test seemed to be measuring what it measured in a consistent manner. In addition, though the test did show some moderate correlations with measures of psychopathology, there were fewer of these, and they were smaller in magnitude than was the case for an earlier developed scale of social desirability. These were promising beginnings for the Marlowe-Crowne Scale but it remained to be shown that the concept of need for approval, and the scale developed to measure it, had a utility beyond predicting responses to other paper-and-pencil measures. Hence, as part of their program of further validating their new scale and the construct that underlay the scale, Crowne, Marlowe, and their students undertook an ingenious series of studies relating scores on their scale to subjects' behavior in a number of nonpaper-and-pencil test situations.

In the first of these studies, subjects began by completing various tests, including the Marlowe-Crowne Scale, and then were asked to get down to the serious business of the experiment itself. That serious business required subjects to (a) pack a dozen spools of thread into a small box, (b) unpack the box, (c) repack the box, (d) reunpack the box, and so on for 25 minutes while the experimenter appeared to be timing the performances and making notes about them. After these dull 25 minutes had elapsed, subjects were asked to rate how interesting the task had been, how instructive, how important to science, and how much the subject wanted to participate in similar experiments in the future. The results of this study showed quite clearly that those subjects who scored above the mean on need for approval said that they found the task more interesting, more instructive, more important to science, and that they were more eager to participate again in similar studies than those subjects who had scored below the mean. Apparently, then, just as we would predict, subjects higher in the need for social approval said nicer things to their high status experimenter about the task and the experiment which he had set for them.

Next, the investigators conducted a series of studies employing the method of verbal conditioning. In one variant of this method, the subject is asked to say all the words he can think of to the listening experimenter. In the positive reinforcement condition, every time the subject utters a plural noun the experimenter says "Mm-hmm" and nods his head. In the negative reinforcement condition, every time the subject utters a plural noun, the experimenter says "Uh-uh." In these methods the magnitude of verbal conditioning is often defined by the increase in the production of plural nouns from the prereinforcement level to some subsequent time block after the subject has received his reinforcements (e.g., head nods). Magnitude of verbal conditioning is often thought to be a good index of a simple type of susceptibility to social influence. Subjects who are more susceptible to the experimenter's reinforcements are thought to be also more susceptible to other forms of elementary social influence.

In the first of their verbal conditioning studies, the investigators found that subjects higher in the need for social approval emitted far more plural nouns when positively reinforced for them than did subjects lower in the need for approval. Similarly, subjects higher in need for approval emitted fewer plural nouns when negatively reinforced for them than did subjects lower in the need for social approval. In this particular experiment, pains were taken to screen out those subjects who saw the connection between their utterances and the experimenter's reinforcement. In this way, the relationship obtained was between subjects' need for approval as measured by the Marlowe-Crowne Scale and subjects' responsivity to the approval of their experimenter but only when they were not explicitly aware of the role of the experimenter's reinforcement.

In the second of their verbal conditioning studies, the investigators wanted to employ a task for subjects that would be more lifelike and more engaging than producing random words. For this purpose, subjects were asked to describe their own personality and every positive self-reference was reinforced by the experimenter's saying "Mm-hmm" in a flat monotone. A positive self-reference was defined as any statement reflecting favorably upon the subject and, despite this seemingly vague definition, two judges working independently showed a very high degree of consistency in identifying positive self-reference. Results of the study showed that subjects above the mean in need for social approval made significantly more positive self-references than did subjects scoring lower in the need for approval. It now appeared that regardless of whether the subjects' responses were as trivial as the production of random words or as meaningful as talking about oneself, these responses could be increased much more by subtle social reinforcement if the subjects were higher in their measured need for social approval.

In their third verbal conditioning study the investigators employed a vicarious reinforcement method. In this procedure the subject is not reinforced for a given type of response, but he is in a position to observe someone else receive reinforcement. The actual subjects of the study observed a pseudosubject, a confederate of the experimenter, make up a series of sentences using one of six pronouns and a verb given him by the experimenter. Whenever the pseudosubject began his sentence with the pronouns "I" or "We," the experimenter said the word "good." Before and after the observation period, subjects themselves made up sentences using one of the same six pronouns. Results of the study showed that subjects higher in need for approval showed a significantly greater increase in their use of "I" and "We" from their preobservational to their postobservational sentence-construction session than did subjects lower in the need for social approval. Thus, once again it was shown that subjects can be successfully predicted to be more responsive to the approving behavior of an experimenter when they have scored higher on a test of the need for approval.

Still another set of studies was undertaken to extend the validity of the Marlowe-Crowne Scale and of the construct of need for approval. This time the method employed was a derivative of a conformity paradigm developed by social psychologist Solomon Asch (1952). In this situation a group of subjects must make judgments on some issue or other. Judgments are announced by each subject, and the purpose of the technique is to permit an assessment of the effects of earlier subjects' judgments on the judgments of subsequent judges. In order to control the earlier-made judgments, accomplices are employed to play the role of subjects, and they usually are all programmed to make the same judgment, one that is quite clearly in error. Conformity is defined as the real subject's going along with the majority in his own judgment rather than giving the objectively correct response.

In Marlowe and Crowne's variation of this paradigm, the subjects listened to a tape recording of knocks on a table and then reported their judgment of the number of knocks they had heard. Each subject was led to believe she was the fourth subject, and she heard the tape-recorded responses of three prior subjects to each series of knocks that were to be judged. The earlier three subjects were, of course, accomplices, and they all agreed with one another by consistently giving an incorrect response on 12 of the 18 trials. For each real subject, then, it was possible to count the number of times out of 12 that she yielded to the wrong but unanimous majority. Results showed that subjects scoring higher in the need for social approval did indeed conform more to the majority judgment than did subjects scoring lower in the need for approval.

In the Asch-type situation employed, the wrong but unanimous majority had not been physically present in the room with the subjects, and the investigators wanted to know whether they would obtain the same results employing "live" accomplices. This time the task was a discrimination problem in which subjects had to judge which of two clusters of dots was larger. Once again, accomplices were employed to give responses that were clearly wrong but that were unanimous. As before, the results showed that subjects scoring above the mean on the need for approval measure yielded more often to the unanimous but erring majority than did the subjects scoring below the mean.

We have now seen a substantial number of studies that support the validity of the Marlowe-Crowne Scale and document the utility of their concept of the need for social approval. There are studies, to be sure, that do not support the investigators' major findings, but there are also additional findings that do. Our purpose here is not to be exhaustive but to document an unusually elegant series of studies that serves well to illustrate the nature of relational research in personality.

EXPERIMENTAL RESEARCH

We speak of experimental research when the investigator has introduced some new feature into the environment for some of the research subjects and then has compared the reaction of these subjects with the reactions of other subjects who have not been exposed to the new feature. In both the OSS assessment program and in the Crowne and Marlowe research program on need for approval, there were many instances in which investigators introduced some new feature, some experimental manipulation, into the situation. Yet, we did not regard those manipulations as exemplifying experimental research because the primary interest was not in the comparison between the behavior of subjects exposed to the new feature and the behavior of subjects not exposed to the new feature.

In the field of personality research there are many investigations that might serve to illustrate the genre of experimental research. It would be difficult, however, to find an example of a more elegant and important program of research than that of Harry Harlow and his collaborators dealing with affection in primates.

There are few personality theories that do not consider early life experiences to be of special importance in the development of personality. Among the early life experiences often given special attention are those involving mother-child relationships. A generally posed proposition might be this one: loving mother-child relationships are more likely to lead to healthy adult personality than hostile, rejecting mother-child relationships. To investigate this proposition experimentally, we would be required to assign half our sample of young children to loving mothers and half to rejecting mothers and follow up the development of the children's adult personality. Such an experimental plan is an ethical absurdity in our culture's value matrix although there are no special problems of experimental logic involved. Does this mean that we can never do experimental work on important questions of human development and human personality? One approach to the problem has capitalized on the biological continuities between infrahuman organisms and man. Primates especially have been shown to share attributes with humans sufficiently to make them valuable, if far from exact or even very accurate, models for man. We cannot, for the sake of furthering our knowledge of personality development, separate a human baby from its mother, but the important lessons we might learn from such separation make it seem justifiable to separate a nonhuman primate from its mother.

In their extensive research program at the University of Wisconsin, the Harlows and their collaborators have employed a great array of the research methods and approaches of both the psychologist and the biologist. Much of their research on the affectional system of monkeys has been of the descriptive type (e.g., young monkeys become attached to other young monkeys) and of the relational type (e.g., male monkeys become more forceful with age; female monkeys become more passive).

Our interest here, however, will focus on their experimental research although we shall be able to describe only a fraction of it.

As part of that research program, infant monkeys were separated from their mothers just a few hours after birth and were raised by bottle with great success. The Harlows had been advised by Dr. Gertrude van Wagenen to have available for their infant monkeys some soft pliant surfaces, and folded gauze diapers were consequently made available to all the baby monkeys. The babies became very much attached to these diapers, so much so that they could only be removed for laundering with great difficulty. These observations led to an experiment designed so that it would show more systematically the shorter- and longer-term effects of access to a soft material. The research was planned also to shed light on the question of the relative importance to the development of the infant's attachment to its mother of being fed by her as opposed to being in close and cuddly contact with her (Harlow, 1959, 1966).

Accordingly, two pseudomothers were built: one a bare, welded-wire cylindrical form with a crude wooden head and face attached, the other a similar apparatus but covered with terry cloth. Eight new-born monkeys were given equal access to the wire-and-cloth mother figures, but four of the monkeys were fed at the breast of the wire mother, and four were fed at the breast of the cloth mother. Results showed that when the measures were of the amount of milk consumed or the amount of weight gained, the two mothers made no difference. The monkeys fed by the two mothers drank about the same amount of milk and gained about the same amount of weight. However, regardless of which mother had fed them, baby monkeys spent much more time climbing up on the cloth mother and clinging to her than they did on the wire mother. This finding was important for a number of reasons; not only for demonstrating the importance of contact comfort but also for showing that a simple earlier formulation of love for mother was really much too simple. That earlier formulation held that mothers became prized because they were associated with the reduction of hunger and thirst. The Harlow results show quite clearly that being the source of food is not nearly as good a predictor of a baby's subsequent preference as is being a soft and cuddly mother. When the monkeys were about 100 days old, they spent an average of about 15 hours a day on the cloth mother but only about 1.5 hours on the wire mother, regardless of whether it had been the cloth or wire mother that had fed the baby monkey.

Later experiments showed that when the infant monkey was placed into a fear-arousing situation, it was the cloth mother that was sought out for comfort and reassurance. A frightened monkey, confronted by a mechanical bear that advanced while beating a drum, would flee to the cloth mother, secure a dose of reassurance, then gradually explore the frightening objects and begin to turn them into toys. When the cloth mother was not in the room, the infant monkeys hurled themselves onto the floor, clutched their heads and bodies, and screamed in distress. The bare-wire mother provided the infant with no greater security or reassurance than did no mother at all.

A collaborator in the Harlow group, Robert A. Butler, had discovered that monkeys enclosed in a dimly lit box would spend hour after hour pressing a lever that would open a window in the box and give them a chance to see something outside. Monkeys barely able to walk will press the lever for a brief peak at the world outside. One of the variables that determines how hard the monkey will work to look out the window is what there is to be seen. When the monkey infants we have been discussing were tested in the "Butler box" it turned out that monkeys worked as hard to see their cloth mothers as to see another real monkey. On the other hand, they worked no harder to see the wire mother than to see nothing at all outside the box. Not only in this experiment, but to a surprising degree in general, a wire mother is not much better than no mother at all, but a cloth mother comes close to being as good as the real thing. Harlow has, however, found other views prevalent among monkey fathers.

A number of female monkeys became mothers themselves although they had not had any monkey mothers of their own and no physical contact with age-mates during the first year of their life (Harlow and Harlow, 1965). Compared to normal monkey mothers, these unmothered mothers were usually brutal to their firstborn offspring, hitting them, kicking them, and crushing them. Those motherless mothers who were not brutal were indifferent. The most cheerful result of this experiment was that those motherless monkeys who went on to become mothers for a second time, treated their second babies in a normal or even an overprotective manner.

A very important series of studies required that infant monkeys be raised in social isolation (Harlow and Harlow, 1970). When the isolation is total the young monkey is exposed to no other living organism; all its physical needs are met in automated fashion, A major independent variable is length of isolation since birth: zero, three, six, or twelve months. All the monkeys raised in isolation were physically healthy, but when placed into a new environment they appeared to crouch in terror. Those monkeys that had been isolated only three months recovered from their neurotic fear within a month or so. Those monkeys that had been isolated for six months never did quite recover.

Their play behavior, even after six months, was minimal and usually isolated. Their social activity, when it did occur, was directed only to monkeys that had also been raised in isolation. Those monkeys that had been isolated for twelve months showed the most severe retardation of play and of the development of aggression. Apathetic and terrified, these monkeys were defenseless against the attacks of the healthy control group monkeys.

Longer-term effects of early social isolation have also been discovered. Several years later, the six-month isolated monkeys showed a dramatic change in orientation to other monkeys. Whereas earlier they had been attacked by other monkeys and had not bothered to defend themselves, they had by now developed into pathological aggressors, attacking other monkeys large and small, acts virtually never occurring among normal monkeys of their age. Another long-term effect of early social isolation can be seen in the inadequacy of the sexual behavior of these monkeys. Even females who were only partially isolated in infancy avoid contact with breeding males, do not groom themselves, engage in threats, in aggression, in clutching themselves, biting themselves, and failing often to support the male should mounting occur. Normal females rarely engage in any of these behaviors. Male monkeys who have been isolated show even more serious sexual inadequacy than do the isolated females. When contrasted with normal males, they groom less, threaten more, are more aggressive, initiate little sex contact, engage in unusual sex behavior, and almost never achieve intromission.

In the extensive research program of the Harlow group, there were many other experiments. Some monkeys were raised without mothers but with access to age-mates while other monkeys were raised by their mothers but without access to age-mates (Harlow and Harlow, 1966). The overall results, while complicated, suggested that both normal mothering and normal age-mate contact are important to normal social development but that to some extent each can substitute for some deficits in the other. Both types of experience are better than either alone, but either alone appears to be very much better than neither.

We have looked now at the research program on the antecedents of affection in monkey babies and adults conducted under Harlow's leadership at Wisconsin. This program illustrates well the power of the experimental method to permit us to make strong inferences of a causal nature. When the same question can be answered by experimental and nonexperimental methods, we usually prefer the former because of the greater strength of causal inference that generally is associated with it. But we often do not have the option open to us, and we conduct research of a descriptive or relational nature because that is all we can conduct. Sometimes we conduct nonexperimental research because that is what seems most urgently needed at that stage of our knowledge in a given area. In this section, we have illustrated each of the three types of research (observational, relational, and experimental) with a relatively recent, yet already classic, example of the genre. Each group of investigators not only conducted outstanding research, but also, in knowing when to employ what type of research, showed wisdom.

chapter three

research variables and causality

CAUSAL INFERENCE

There was a time when it was routinely the custom to deal in chapters like this with the concept of causality. Perhaps wisely, perhaps overcautiously, behavioral researchers have taken to sidestepping the issues involved in defining causality. We hear more nowadays of "antecedents," "determinants," "independent variables," and other such terms that allow one to creep up on the notion of causality without getting oneself in trouble with colleagues from philosophy, although the writings of some of the best of them suggest we have nothing to fear and, indeed, something to learn—for example, Kaplan's (1964) *The Conduct of Inquiry*. Though the term causality has suffered from a loss of popularity, the idea of wanting to know what leads to what is as popular today as ever and may be seen as the heart of the business of science.

More commonly, of course, we say that "understanding" is the goal of science; but we need only push a bit to see that understanding is a quite subjective matter. I understand a certain phenomenon and if you don't see it my way, why then you simply don't understand it. But perhaps I can show you I understand a phenomenon by making predictions about what will happen in the future, predictions based on my understanding of the phenomenon in which we are interested. If we disagree in our understandings, then perhaps you will also want to make some predictions based on your understanding. If your understanding logically implies predictions that are better borne out by the observations we make than are my predictions based on my understanding, then I am willing to concede your greater understanding of the phenomenon in question.

Wanting to know what leads to what suggests the need for experimental observation. Perhaps the only way to be sure that X leads to Y is to vary X experimentally and observe the consequences. Compared to the nonexperimental relational observation, the experimental observation is vastly preferable. It permits a stronger inference that it must have been X that led to Y, and while X may still be a fearfully complicated set of events we have brought about, we are, nevertheless, confident that, at least, X was not brought about by Y.

Sometimes, of course, it is not possible to conduct an experiment for ethical or for technical reasons, and then we are glad to fall back onto our nonexperimental relational observations. Suppose, for example, that we had discovered an outbreak of strange psychological symptoms among several hundred people all over the country. We might begin our efforts to understand the problem by interviewing some or all of the afflicted with the descriptive aim of telling something of what these people could have in common. Our interviews, let us say, suggest that all the people with the strange psychological symptoms had recently visited a physician and that they had all had prescribed for them a new drug whose side effects were not yet fully established.

Now we suspect that the drug may for some persons at least be the determinant of the strange psychological symptoms. From what we have said before, is an experiment not needed? Shall we take a random sample of people visiting physicians and arrange to give half of them the suspected drug? That would allow us to conclude whether those given the drug were more likely to develop the strange psychological symptoms, but the cost of such research would be too high. We would not be willing to expose people to a drug we had good reason to believe to be harmful. As an alternative, we might do as sophisticated a job as possible of employing nonexperimental relational observations. We might want to compare those persons who were given the new drug by their physicians with those persons whose physicians did not prescribe the new drug. If only those given the new drug developed the new symptoms, the new drug would be more seriously implicated, but its determining role would still not be fully established. It might have been, for example, that those persons given the new drug differed in a number of ways from those who were not given the drug by their physicians. Not the new drug, then, but a correlate of being given the new drug might be the determining factor.

Other analyses are possible that might help us to judge whether the new drug is a determinant of the new symptom. Among those patients given the new drug some will very likely have been given large dosages while others will have been given small dosages. If it turns out that persons on larger dosages suffer more severely from the new symptoms, the new drug will be more strongly implicated. Once again, however, we cannot be certain about the antecedent role of the drug. It might be the case, for example, that those who are judged to be more ill by the physician are given larger dosages so that it is the illness for which the drug is prescribed that is the effective agent rather than the drug itself.

Despite the difficulty of clear inference in the absence of experimental observations, most scientists are willing to be convinced by strong evidence even if fairly indirect. Thus, if persons taking the drug are more likely to show the symptoms, if those taking more of the drug show more of the symptoms, and if those taking it over a longer period of time show more of the symptoms, a prudent man would be cautious about deciding that the drug was not a determinant of the symptoms. Even if an investigator were not willing to conclude that the drug were surely at the root of the symptoms, at least not on the basis of the type of evidence outlined, he might well decide that it would be wisest to act as though it were.

A more direct and compelling demonstration of causality—that X did, in fact, produce Y—would require that at least three principal types of evidence be brought to bear. First, it should be shown that X actually was a contributory condition of Y. If the mysterious malaise occurred only among those patients who had been administered the drug and not among any others, this would be evidence of a concomitant variation, proof that the relation of X and Y was invariant. While this implies, in effect, that the drug was both a necessary and sufficient condition for the odd psychological symptoms, the drug could also be merely the culmination of a set of sufficient conditions. For example, in order to be susceptible to the drug a person might already have to be in a given anticipatory state of distress. In other than experimental research, this could be a difficult alternative to rule out because of the potential danger that subjects were "self-selected" into the research groups because they possessed characteristics that were indirectly related to the problem. The second bit of evidence bearing on causal inference would be proof that Y did not occur until after X had been set into operation. Thus, it would have to be shown that none of the victims showed these symptoms before the drug was administered. Finally, there should also be evidence to rule out any other plausible determining conditions.

RESEARCH VARIABLES

It is a convenience to be able to refer somewhat abstractly to the things we would like to investigate, and the convention is to call them variables.

What is called the dependent variable refers to the behavioral response in which one is interested—in the example just given, the dependent variable is the presence or absence of the malaise, or what was symbolized by Y. Thus, dependent variables are also sometimes referred to as response variables, the idea, which derives from the semantics of causality, being that they are the effects of identifiable causes.

What is called the independent variable refers to the factors upon which the dependent variable depends, or X in the hypothetical illustration given. Hence, changes in the independent variable are thought to lead to changes in the dependent variable. In the example, initially we were not at all sure what the independent variable was, although interviewing the afflicted—a variation of the case-study approach—led us to hypothesize that it could have something to do with a drug that they had all had prescribed for them. Employing once again the language of causality, all "causes" would be independent variables (although many independent variables would not be thought of as causes).

In practice it is not always so easy to distinguish independent variables from dependent variables. The distinction is easiest to make when the research is based on experimental observations. In that case, one has established clear control by producing the independent variable himself. Examples were seen in Table 3, where one finds Harlow's independent variable to be the softness of a monkey-mother, Milgram's independent variable to be the distance between the potential givers and receivers of electric shock, and Matarazzo, Wiens, and Saslow's independent variable to be the average length of the interviewer's utterances. The dependent variable in each of these three experiments are preference for one over the other mother, amount of electric shock administered to the victim, and length of the applicants' utterances.

While it is difficult to be confused about the independent and dependent variables in experimental relational research, it is sometimes quite easy to be confused about them in nonexperimental research. Thus, in Milgram's research, is it the subjects' tension that is the independent variable leading to their greater willingness to apply electric shock, or is this willingness itself the independent variable affecting the subjects' tension level? Similar difficulties of decision are to be found in the other examples of Table 2. Do smaller baboon groups go higher up the mountainside, so that group size is the independent variable, or do groups living higher up lose more members so that location is the independent variable? Is psychological stability the independent variable affecting speech duration, or is speech duration the independent variable affecting the extent to which people are judged as psychologically stable?

Sometimes, when there is doubt about the dependence of a variable, the logical temporal sequence can be a possible basis for decision. Thus, in examining the relationship between sex and height we feel that sex is more likely to determine height than that height is to determine sex. Similarly, in examining the relationship between birth order and volunteering to participate in certain psychological experiments, we think of birth order as the independent variable because it does not seem reasonable to think that volunteering to participate in a psychological experiment might be a determinant of one's order of birth. Sex and birth order, then, are likely to be called independent variables because they are determined so early in the history of the organism.

Ordinarily when we speak of dependent variables we mean that they are dependent relative to one or more independent variables. There are occasions, however, when we are not interested at all in what is likely to lead to what. In such cases we may want only to know how two variables are related, with no implication of one serving as determinant, "cause," or even antecedent, of the other. If we want only to know the relationship, for example, between two measures of racial prejudice, or authoritarianism, or IQ, we refer to them as variables but would not usually try to distinguish independent from dependent variables.

KINDS OF INDEPENDENT VARIABLES

We have implied that it is not always so easy to specify the independent variable when studying the antecedents of some behavioral change, to know precisely what X and not—X. We return to this point later when we consider a peculiarity of human behavioral research that can further complicate the issue. In general, however, a researcher will usually focus on a particular independent variable because of its theoretical significance to the problem in which he is interested. If one is concerned about why people don't help others in an emergency, he might, as Latané and Darley did in their research discussed in Chapter 1, emphasize the sheer number of witnesses to the crisis. Factors like the victim's need for social approval or the helper's genetic inheritance should not be at all related to the diffusion-of-responsibility hypothesis and, therefore, would be very unlikely to appear as independent variables in research stimulated by this idea. Depending also on the researcher's training in his scientific discipline, some independent variables may be favored over others merely from force of habit. Thus, most sociologists and anthropologists will tend to stress the social and cultural environment over other possible independent variables; psychophysiologists, biological factors; educational researchers, previous training and experience. The more kinds of theoretically relevant independent variables that are tapped, the more generality and applicability can the research findings have and the more precisely can the relationship between X and Y be stated.

Since it will be inconvenient or impossible most times, either for economic or logical reasons, to study all the relevant independent variables in just a single investigation, a program of studies—Harlow's baby monkey studies are an example—can be developed in which variations of the independent variable(s) are introduced from experiment to experiment. In this way, by the attempted systematic replication of the original experimental conditions, it should also be possible to determine the real limits to an inferred causal relationship. Thus, an initial study of the diffusion-of-responsibility hypothesis might simply vary the number of people who were witnesses to an emergency. A follow-up study, using the same experimental paradigm, could systematically introduce as an additional independent variable the racial similarity between victim and witnesses, or perhaps use male and female witnesses, or systematically replicate the original study in different cultures or with different kinds of emergencies. Any number of interesting combinations of independent variables is possible, and each successful systematic replication will ensure greater confidence in the preceding empirical relationships.

What are the kinds of independent variables from which to choose? There are many possible ways of classifying independent variables. For example, one might think of internal factors that can "push" an organism in a particular direction or toward a specific goal or object. His need for social approval, his biological drives, a given hereditary predisposition—all of these might be internally operative independent variables worth exploring. In contrast, the organism might be "pulled" by external conditions: aspects of the social environment, group pressures, societal mores. Of course, he could be both "pulled" and "pushed," and it might be well worth exploring both kinds of independent variables.

Another way of grouping independent variables could be in the plausible duration of their influence. Short-term variables—for example, those affecting compliance with the law—should have a momentary effect in raising or lowering this tendency. The immediate presence of sight, but they exerted no extra effort to replenish the supply by going to the refrigerator for more. Thus, for the obese at least, appetite was probably determined by the independent variable of the amount of food immediately available to them. While the factor of the subjects' weight, or overweight, might be grouped in the first class of independent variables because of its biological link, the number of roast beef sandwiches can be seen as a social-environmental independent variable.

Social environment, the second kind of independent variable, taps a whole host of assorted elements. The physical setting of the research study, whether subjects are left alone or in groups, whether some are occupied with another task and others are not—one might very easily construct hypotheses for the plausible operation of each of these social factors in the case of eating behavior. For instance, reading while eating roast beef sandwiches might be a distracting enough element that it turned a normal eater's attention away from what he was consuming and thus led him to eat much more than usual. An extremely unappetizing physical setting should slow down even the heartiest eater. In the presence of others—following Zajonc's social facilitation principle—eating behavior, being a well-learned response, might be facilitated.

The third class of independent variables is heredity, or factors associated with the subject's genetic endowment. In many cases, there might be a close link between this class of independent variable and the class of biological independent variables. Wilkins and Richter (1940) described the case of a child born with a cortico-adrenal insufficiency who showed an enormous and continual craving for salt. His malfunctioning adrenals were not discovered until his death, however. Brought by his perplexed parents to the hospital to find a cure for his unusual salt-raiding drive, the unsuspecting dietician kept the child on a normal hospital diet and he died within a few days. His great appetite for salt, unbeknownst to his poor parents, was what had been instrumental in keeping him alive.

Previous training and experience constitute the fourth class of independent variables. For example, experiments by Rozin (1967, 1969) have shown that rats maintained on a diet that is deficient in thiamine will prefer one that is supplemented by this vitamin over one that is not. However, he has also shown that the behavior is learned, not innate. The rat eats the more favorable diet because of its more favorable consequences, not because he necessarily "knows" what is good for him. Given a choice of several diets, only one of which contains the nutrient he lacks, the hungry rat will consume one of the diets for several days until its effect is felt. If it is not a healthy diet, he will

a policeman could, in some circumstances, be a stimulus
the law (e.g., hitting the brakes upon spying the highw
at work), and in others, a sufficient reason *for* breaking
mob of demonstrators who feel provoked or frustrated by
of the police). Long-term variables, such as social norms
role expectations, should be more stable and less likely to

Another workable scheme for clarifying independent
whether it is a biological drive, an aspect of the social
a hereditary factor, something having to do with previous
experience, or the element of maturity. While the five cla
pendent variables may be exhaustive, they are certainly n
exclusive. To illustrate, consider a collection of research
the question of eating behavior.

The first kind of independent variable is the biolo
Drive refers to the increase of energy that is available to
as a result of a state of need having been aroused—hunger,
sex are examples of basic biological needs. By comparing
that were in a state of deprivation with regard to food v
who were already quite satiated on food, the independent
variable of the organism's hunger drive could be studied f
on any given dependent variable. If one wanted to study
an independent variable, he could take a matched sample of
nonobese subjects and submit them to a special situation
their different reactions (the dependent variable) could be
Healthy obese and nonobese rats might, for example, be s
electrical stimulation of the brain in order to determine
foundations of their eating behavior. Nisbett (1968) did
study in which there were two independent variables: on
subject's weight and the other was the amount of food mad
to him. Nisbett wanted to see whether appetite for a languis
mand might not also be determined by how much food was
him. College students were divided into three groups depe
whether they were overweight, of normal weight, or underwe
student was then left alone to eat roast beef sandwiches. Half t
in each group were offered one sandwich to begin with, and t
three sandwiches, although they all were told to help ther
more if they liked as there were other sandwiches in a refrig
the next room. For the normal males, each ate about two sa
and it made no difference whether the original offer was for
beef sandwich or three. Those in the one-sandwich conditi
therefore, have gone to the refrigerator for more, whereas tho
three-sandwich condition must have eaten one sandwich less t
was offered to them. In contrast, the obese subjects ate ever

experiment with another, and so on until he learns which diet has the most favorable consequences.

The fifth class of independent variables is maturity. Because age is a variable that can be closely associated with all the other classes of independent variables, even in the most thoughtful and well-reasoned analysis it may not always be possible to specify whether it was the organism's maturity or some other, related variable that was the source of the observed effect. If it were found that very old and very young human beings tended to consume less food than others, would it be because of their chronological age, the reduced potency of a biological drive, or because of societal expectations and the more limited availability of or access to food? There is not always a clear distinction on what exactly are X and not—X.

KINDS OF DEPENDENT VARIABLES

Selecting the dependent variable is also sometimes a matter of convention and accessibility, although it is always better dictated on theoretical grounds for its relevance to the scientific problem under investigation. Also, just as the tapping of several kinds of theoretically relevant independent variables can increase the generality and applicability of a set of research findings, so can the observation of different dependent variables (along with the repeated observation of the same dependent variable) increase the scientific value of the data by showing the limits and persistence of the inferred $X–Y$ relationship.

If one were interested in assessing the behavioral effects of emotional and rational propaganda, he could observe how much attitude change occurred in subjects exposed to each communication, and this would tell something of the potency of the propaganda. He would probably also want to measure the direction of the attitude changes to determine if there were any boomerang effects. If he observed the attitudes repeatedly over a period of time, this could tell him how long the changes lasted and whether there was a sleeper effect. When taken altogether, the observations would reveal a great deal about the limits and durability of the effects of the two types of propaganda.

What are the kinds of behavioral changes that can serve as dependent variables? We can speak of (a) the direction of change, (b) the quantity or persistence of change, and (c) the ease with which changes are effected. In an animal-learning experiment, where the paradigm might consist of teaching a thirsty rat to run to one or another end of a complicated maze for a small thimbleful of water, the dependent variable could be (a) the direction he chose on each trial, whether it was always to the right or always to the left, (b) how long he persisted in the correct response when the water was no longer available at the end of his run and all that greeted him each time was an empty thimble, and (c) the ease with which he reacquired the correct response when the thimble of water was again made available to him.

A rather different way of grouping behavioral dependent variables has been suggested by Uriel Foa (1968). One kind of behavioral change refers to a diffusion, or irradiation, of the behavioral effect of one variable toward other responses that are close in time to the central change. The things-go-better-with-Coke effect, mentioned in Chapter 1 as an illustration of the rule-of-thumb approach for constructing hypotheses, can be interpreted in this way. Treating someone to a tasty lunch is a time-tested method for salesmen to soften up their client for the sales pitch. The positively toned feeling about eating seems to become "diffused" to, or transferred onto, an entirely different dependent variable, but that is close in time to the eating response. A series of studies on this spread-of-effect phenomenon as it influences attitude changes has shown that one can shift attitudes in a specified direction by exposing people to propaganda in the course of an emotionally satisfying or dissatisfying experience; persons who are exposed to both sides of an issue should tend to shift their opinions in the direction of whichever side was presented more closely in time to an emotionally satisfying experience or farther in time, within reasonable limits, from a dissatisfying one (Rosnow, 1968, 1972). For example, one such study dealt with the attitudes of some high school students toward the work of Pablo Picasso (Corrozi and Rosnow, 1968). Four sets of arguments were prepared; two were pro-and-con positions on the genius of Picasso. Two were pro-and-con positions on the question, "Should we have a longer school week?" The experiment consisted of exposing groups of students to both Picasso arguments in conjunction with one or the other of the school-week arguments, varying the sequence and timing of presentation, and measuring the resulting shifts of opinion. On correlating the results, it was found that the argument against a longer school week put students in a frame of mind highly receptive to whichever Picasso argument accompanied it more closely in time, and conversely, that the argument in favor of a longer school week caused students to be more receptive to the Picasso argument that was presented farther away in time.

A second kind of behavioral change concerns alterations in the degrees of relationship among people. If we wanted to study the effects of different communication networks on aspects of problem-solving behavior in groups, we might try different patterns and observe what changes occurred that affected the behavior of the group. Was the speed of solution of the problem increased or decreased? Did solutions become any more or less accurate? What were the effects on morale that could alter the cohesiveness of the group? Three popular communication networks are the circle (where a member may communicate with the person to his left and right), the chain (where communications must travel up and down a hierarchy of command), and the v,heel (where one central member may communicate with all the other members).

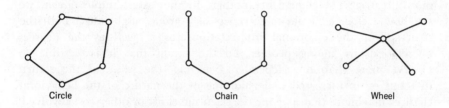

Circle   Chain   Wheel

The wheel typically provides the fastest speed of solution and greatest accuracy, and the circle is usually the slowest and least accurate. By contrast, morale is usually best in a circle communication network and poorest in a wheel network (Bavelas, 1950; Collins and Raven, 1969; Leavitt, 1951).

A third kind of change is the structural reorganization of interrelationships. In group psychotherapy this may be a common occurrence as the cohesiveness of the interrelationships is influenced. For example, the marathon group is a continuous meeting, lasting as long as three or four uninterrupted days. It provides an intensive experience in group process, often with momentarily dramatic results. A recent innovation has been to introduce nudity of the members, on the expectation that this will make it easier for people to give up their defenses. If situational changes produced changes in the emotional relationships between people, or if the relationships changed as a function of the duration of the marathon meeting, so would the overall group structure be affected. Thus, person A increases his liking for person C and decreases his liking for person B, and so the structure ABC may change to ACB. One might also imagine changes occurring in the hierarchy of needs of people. For example, Maslow (1962) postulated a motive hierarchy in which hunger, thirst, and similar physiologically based drives were seen to be the most basic needs and where the highest need on the hierarchy was self-actualization, characterized by a superior perception of reality, an increased self-acceptance, increased spontaneity, and autonomy. For a person to achieve this highest psychological state, it was assumed that all his other needs must first be satisfied. Thus, the basic physiological needs could not be wanting, nor could intermediate motives on the hierarchy such as the need for safety, the need for love and belonging, and the need for esteem. The needs in Maslow's hierarchy cannot be automatically fixed as to their intensity and sequence, and their structural order could depend on cultural factors, personal experiences, and many other independent variables (cf. Lana and Rosnow, 1972, pp. 136 ff.).

These various classes of dependent variables are not mutually exclusive, and indeed a change in one kind of behavior might automatically trigger a change in another. In the last examples given, we saw how a change in the cohesiveness of a group might affect both the structure of the emotional interrelationships as well as the degrees of relationship among people. To the extent that it is possible to observe more than one dependent variable, the value of the return in terms of an increased understanding of the nature of the behavioral changes may more than pay for the scientific effort or other cost involved.

chapter four

experimental designs and the concept of controls

CONTROLS IN BEHAVIORAL RESEARCH

The concept of control is quite central to all the sciences, and it has recently received an especially elegant treatment by the late Edwin Boring (1969). At one time the word control meant *counter-roll*, which was a master list used to check and to correct other lists. Control, then, came to mean a check or a control on quality. In science, Boring tells us, the word control has had four meanings, all of which are still useful.

Constancy of Conditions

This sense of control refers to the importance of maintaining those conditions that affect the variables of the research at those levels or values at which we want them or at which we believe them to be. Although we might at some time want to study the effect of temperature variation on human behavior, it would not be thought to be good practice to allow the temperature in our laboratory to vary capriciously from very chilly to very hot. If we let that occur, we would not be able to claim the constancy of conditions that allows statements of relationships to be made with precision.

Control Series

This sense of control refers to the calibration of various elements of the research, including in some cases the apparatus employed and in other cases, even the subjects' mental set. For example, in psychophysical research subjects may be asked to judge whether their skin is being touched by one or two fine compass points. If subjects know that two points will always be applied, they may never report the sensation of being stimulated by only one point. Yet, we know that when two points are sufficiently close to one another they are invariably perceived as only one point. In this situation a control series might consist of applying only one point on a certain percentage of the trials.

Behavioral Control

This sense of the term refers to control over the conditions leading to behavior change and has been used in such applied realms as psychotherapy and education. B. F. Skinner's (1971, 1972) use of this idea in connection with the shaping of behavior is familiar to most of us.

Control Group

This sense of control refers to the employment of a comparison group that is *not* given whatever the experimental group *is* given. Boring gives an early example of a control group in which the independent variable was tetanus immunization and the dependent variable was death. An immunized (experimental) group of rats was compared to an unimmunized (control) group of rats after both had been exposed to tetanus. Rats that had been immunized lived, and rats that had not been immunized died. Note that it was the experimental condition of immunization that was being controlled and not the introduction of tetanus. The effects of the introduction of tetanus were so well known even in this turn-of-the-century research, that it was not necessary to check whether death would be due to the introduction of tetanus instead of, for example, to the injection of some more benign substance.

It is this last sense of the term "control" that is most closely and specifically linked to experimental observations and to the ideas embodied in John Stuart Mill's joint method of agreement and difference. Mill's method is easy to set down:

If X, then Y.
If not—X, then not—Y.

The first line tells us that whenever X occurs, Y will follow. It states that X is sufficient as a determinant of Y, but it takes the addition of the second line to assure us that X is also necessary to bring Y about.

Suppose, for example, that X represents a new and highly touted tranquilizer that can be obtained without prescription, while Y represents a decrease in measured tension. Suppose further that we have a group of subjects who complain of tension, that they take a certain dosage of tranquilizer X and then show a reduction in tension. If X, then Y. But could we conclude from this observation that it was the tranquilizer that led to the reduction in tension?

Suppose we had a control group of equivalent subjects who were not given any pills, and suppose that they did not show any tension reduction. Could we now conclude that taking the drug had led to tension reduction? Yes, we could, but with the clear knowledge that "taking the drug" means something quite different from getting a certain chemical into the blood system.

"Taking the drug" means among other things: (a) having someone give the subject a pill, (b) having someone give the subject the attention that goes with pill giving, (c) having the subject believe that he is taking relevant medication, and (d) having the ingredients of the drug find their way to the blood system of the subject. Usually when testing a new drug one is interested only in the active ingredients. One does not care to learn that subjects will get to feeling better if they believe they are being helped, because this fact is already known. But if one knows this, then how is one to separate the effects of the drug's ingredients from the effects of pill giving, subject expectations of help, and other such psychological variables? We can do it by the choice of a different control group. This time we will employ not a group given nothing but instead a group given something that differs only in terms of the ingredients whose effects we would like to learn. The need for this type of control is so well established in drug research that virtually all trained investigators routinely employ so-called placebo-control groups. The general finding is, incidentally, that placebos are often effective and sometimes even as effective as the far more expensive drug for which they serve as the relevant control.

In our tranquilizer research we first employed a no-pill control group and then a placebo, or sugar pill, control group. Assuming that there is often a choice of control groups, how does one decide on the most appropriate control group? That question is not a simple one, but two of the major factors to be considered in attempting to answer are (a) the specific question of greatest interest to the investigator and (b) what is known generally about the research area in question. Even a very experienced research scientist may go astray in his choice of control groups when he makes a major shift of research areas. Only experience in a given research area is likely to protect the investigator from overlooking an important control group.

THE SOLOMON DESIGN

We can illustrate the complexity of the problem very well by considering a four-group research design developed by Richard L. Solomon (1949) that he and Michael Lessac (1968; Lessac and Solomon, 1969) subsequently applied in a study of the effects of isolating organisms on their later adaptive behavior. Because the Solomon design becomes very complicated when there are multiple independent variables operating, it has only been recommended for experiments where there is one type of identifiable difference between experimental and control groups.

Previous research by other psychological investigators had led to the development of what is called the critical-period hypothesis. This view states that there must be optimum periods in the life of a human or an animal during which it learns how to make adaptive responses to its environment. Withholding various kinds of stimulation early in the organism's development should, it was assumed, impede the learning of sensory and motor associations important to adult behavior. Solomon and Lessac challenged this assumption because it ignores two rival possibilities: first, that the early deprivation destroys an already formed behavioral organization, not one that has yet to form, or second, that the early deprivation creates unusual patterns of responding that simply interfere with the later behaviors.

To rule out these alternatives, it is necessary (a) to pretest the organism's behavior before it is subjected to a state of isolation and (b) at the same time to control for the effects of this required pretesting. In other words, by pretesting the organism, one can later show whether any effects of the isolation were merely a passive arrest of learning processes or an active impediment to existing perceptual-motor patterns. However, since the pretesting might, theoretically at least, serve to enrich the experience of the supposedly deprived subjects, it is necessary to devise a logical means of determining its influence as well. For these purposes, the research design in Table 5 was developed. The design calls for two experimental groups, I and II, and two control groups,

Table 5.   The Solomon Four-Group Research Design

Procedure	Experimental Conditions	
	Isolation	No Isolation
Pretesting	I	III
No pretesting	II	IV

III and IV, the subjects being assigned to each on a purely random basis. Group I is pretested on whatever dependent variables are theoretically relevant, then subjected to a state of isolation, and finally tested once again on the dependent variables. Group II is not pretested, but undergoes the same isolation treatment and is given the same posttests as in Group I. Group III is pretested and posttested, but is treated normally instead of being subjected to a period of isolation. Group IV only gets the posttests.

In carrying out this experiment, beagle puppies were the subjects studied (Lessac and Solomon, 1969). Those assigned to Groups III and IV were reared normally in the same way that they would have been reared in a kennel, and those assigned to Groups I and II were raised in isolation in $18 \times 24 \times 30$-inch aluminum cages through which light entered by a $2\frac{1}{2}$-inch space between the bottom tray and the door. All the puppies were fed and medicated at the same times, and the dependent variables—the measures of which included testing each one's response to pain, how it responded to its physical environment, and various tests of learning—were observed for all groups after one year had passed.

What can the four-group design tell us in this case? First, by averaging the pretest performances of Groups I and III we can infer approximately what the initial performances would have been in Groups II and IV since the subjects, having been assigned at random, each had an equal chance of being assigned to any particular group. Second, we can now examine the posttest performance in Group II without having contaminated it by the pretesting procedures. Thus, a comparison of the inferred mean pretest score in Group II with its actual mean posttest score would enable us to decide whether the isolation produced a deterioration in performance, an improvement, or if it had no effect at all, relative to Group IV. Third, by comparing the posttested scores in Groups I and IV with those in Groups II and III, we can determine the effects of the pretesting on the response to the treatment by applying the formula: $I - (II + III - IV)$. A positive difference score would suggest that the pretesting had an enriching effect; a negative score would suggest the opposite. In the case of the study by Lessac and Solomon, the four-group design enabled them to conclude that behavioral development may not merely be retarded by isolation but, in fact, distorted.

Other specialized control group designs have been developed for a number of different purposes. Thus, there is a good deal of evidence to suggest that in behavioral research the expectancy or hypothesis of the investigator can sometimes function as a self-fulfilling prophecy. That is, experimenters may sometimes communicate to their subjects how they expect them to respond, and this communication can be quite subtle and unintentional (Rosenthal, 1966; 1969). A number of strategies have been developed to minimize these effects of the experimenters' expectancies. One of these strategies involves the use of expectancy control groups (Rosenthal, 1966, Chapter 23). This procedure requires that a given experiment be repeated by several experimenters some of whom expect to find a difference between the experimental and control groups and some of whom do not. If both groups of experimenters obtain the same difference between the experimental and control groups we can be fairly sure that the differences obtained are "real" and not due to the expectancies of the experimenters. However, if the experimenters who expect to find a difference find one, and those who don't expect to find a difference do not, we may conclude that the differences found between groups may be due as much to the effects of the experimenters' expectancies as to any intrinsic difference between the experimental and control groups. When expectancy control groups have been employed they have shown that experimental results can indeed be due primarily to the effects of the experimenters' expectancies (Cooper, Eisenberg, Robert, and Dohrenwend, 1967).

The fact that the employment of more than one control group is possible in arranging to make experimental observations suggests that investigators must make decisions about the specific control groups as well as the experimental group that are to be included in the research. Particularly in some of its more statistical aspects, the design of experiments is a very specialized and highly developed field of its own, a field that behavioral scientists often turn to for advice and guidance. We now discuss three basic designs and ideas that are known generally to researchers and which are employed in the vast majority of behavioral experiments.

FULLY RANDOMIZED DESIGNS

These are research plans in which there are two or more groups to be compared on the dependent variable and the subjects are placed in their particular group at random so that no sampling bias can enter into their assignment to experimental conditions. The procedure has a long scientific history. Frederick II of Hohenstaufen is reported to have used a variation of the design in his grotesque studies in physiology and anatomy. In one experiment, he is supposed to have fed two men a sumptuous dinner and then (presumably at random) sent one to sleep and the other to exercise. After a sufficient interval, each was opened to enable Frederick to observe which had digested better. An older example is the story of how citron was discovered by the ancient

Egyptians to be an antidote for poison (Jones, 1964). It seems that a magistrate had sentenced some convicted criminals to be executed by exposing them to poisonous snakes. However, it was reported back to him that none of the criminals had died despite the care in carrying out the sentence. On inquiring further into the matter, he learned that the criminals, just before they had been exposed to the snakes, were given some citron to eat by an old woman who took pity on them. Hypothesizing that it must be the citron that had saved them, the magistrate directed that the sentence be carried out again, but this time he had the criminals divided into pairs, and he fed citron (again presumably at random) to one of each pair and not to the other. Sure enough, when the criminals were exposed again to the poisonous snakes, the ones who had eaten the citron suffered no harm while the untreated members died instantly. These stories illustrate not only the early use of randomization ideas but the early use of control groups as well.

For a more contemporary, behavioral illustration of the fully randomized research design, assume that we wanted to learn the effect of a hot lunch on the scholastic achievement of ghetto children. Suppose that we did not want to assign children at random to the hot-lunch or not hot-lunch conditions but to let their teachers do the assigning. It might well happen that teachers would in some way choose those children for the hot-lunch condition who would have gained the most in scholastic achievement even without the hot-lunch program. Or, the teachers might have chosen the children who would have gained the least, no matter what experimental conditions were applied.

If such a bias had crept into our assignment of subjects to research conditions, then the hot lunchers would have differed from nonhot lunchers in two respects, one that we wanted them to differ in (lunch versus no lunch) and one that we did not want them to differ in (teacher selection bias). In order to assess the effect of a treatment condition, we want it to differ from a comparison or control condition in only that single systematic respect that we have arranged for experimentally.

Suppose now that we have conducted an experiment on the effects of nutrition on the academic performance of ghetto children, employing four groups or conditions—not the Solomon design but another four-group randomized design. One group of randomly assigned children gets a hot lunch daily, another group gets free milk, a third group gets a vitamin supplement, and the fourth group gets nothing extra. Imagine, now, two different sets of results of this experiment. What conclusions would we be willing to draw on the basis of results A of Table 6 compared to results B? We note for both sets of results that the academic performance of the group receiving no special nutritional

Table 6.   Some Hypothetical Effects of Nutrition on the Academic Performance of Twelve Subjects

	Treatment Conditions			
	Group I Zero	Group II Milk	Group III Vitamins	Group IV Hot Lunch
Alternative results A	$S_1 = 8$ $S_5 = 10$ $S_9 = 12$	$S_2 = 10$ $S_6 = 12$ $S_{10} = 14$	$S_3 = 13$ $S_7 = 15$ $S_{11} = 17$	$S_4 = 17$ $S_8 = 19$ $S_{12} = 21$
	Sum = 30	Sum = 36	Sum = 45	Sum = 57
	Mean = 10	Mean = 12	Mean = 15	Mean = 19
Alternative results B	$S_1 = 4$ $S_5 = 10$ $S_9 = 16$	$S_2 = 6$ $S_6 = 12$ $S_{10} = 18$	$S_3 = 9$ $S_7 = 15$ $S_{11} = 21$	$S_4 = 13$ $S_8 = 19$ $S_{12} = 25$
	Sum = 30	Sum = 36	Sum = 45	Sum = 57
	Mean = 10	Mean = 12	Mean = 15	Mean = 19

bonus, Group I, was 10 units of academic performance, on the average. Also, on the average, the group receiving milk (Group II) scored 12, that receiving vitamins (Group III) scored 15 on the average while that receiving hot lunches (Group IV) scored an average of 19 points. Since the average performance of each of the four groups was the same for the two sets of results, will we not draw the same conclusions from both sets of results? Perhaps we would draw generally the same conclusion that hot lunches seem more effective than vitamins, which themselves are more effective than milk, which seems to be somewhat better than nothing. However, results in A, when compared carefully to results B, seem to be more convincing on some intuitive basis. In results A, subjects never varied in their performance by more than two points from the average score of their group while subjects in results B varied as much as six points from the average score of their group.

The few points worth of difference between the average, or mean, scores of the four groups look larger when seen against the background of the small within-group variation of results A, while they look smaller when seen against the background of the large within-group variation of results B. A more formal comparison of the variation between the average results per condition and the average variation within the different conditions is possible and is called an analysis of variance. In such an analysis a ratio is formed with the variance of group means from one another divided by the variance of individual scores from the means of their particular conditions. Called an F ratio, it will have a value close to unity (1.00) when the variation between conditions is not different from the variation within conditions. The larger the F ratio becomes, the greater is the dispersion of group means relative to the dispersion of scores within groups and the less likely it becomes that the dispersion among group means could easily have occurred by chance.

The numerator of the F ratio (dispersion among condition means) is defined as:

$$\frac{T_1{}^2/n_1 + T_2{}^2/n_2 + \cdots + T_a{}^2/n_a - (\text{Total})^2/N}{a - 1}$$

where

$T_1 =$ the sum of the scores of the first group
$T_2 =$ the sum of the scores of the second group
$T_a =$ the sum of the scores of the ath or last group
$n_1 =$ the number of cases or scores of the first group
$n_2 =$ the number of cases or scores of the second group
$n_a =$ the number of cases or scores of the ath or last group
$N =$ the number of cases or scores added over all groups
$\text{Total} =$ the sum of the scores added over all groups
$a =$ the number of groups being compared

Results A and results B of Table 6 have identical numerators for their respective variance ratios:

$$\frac{(30)^2/3 + (36)^2/3 + \cdots + (57)^2/3 - (168)^2/12}{4 - 1} = \frac{138}{3} = 46$$

The denominator of the F ratio (dispersion within conditions) is defined as:

$$\frac{X_1{}^2 + X_2{}^2 + \cdots + X_N{}^2 - T_1{}^2/n_1 - T_2{}^2/n_2 - \cdots - T_a{}^2/n_a}{N - a}$$

where X_1 is the first individual score, X_2 the second individual score, and X_N the Nth or last individual score.

Result A of Table 6, then, has the following denominator for the F ratio:

$$\frac{(8)^2 + (10)^2 + \cdots + (21)^2 - (30)^2/3 - (36)^2/3 - \cdots - (57)^2/3}{12 - 4} = \frac{32}{8} = 4,$$

while result B of Table 6 has the denominator:

$$\frac{(4)^2 + (6)^2 + \cdots + (25)^2 - (30)^2/3 - (36)^2/3 - \cdots - (57)^2/3}{12 - 4}$$

$$= \frac{288}{8} = 36,$$

a result that makes the F ratio ($\frac{46}{36} = 1.28$) for results B only one-ninth the size of the F ratio ($\frac{46}{4} = 11.50$) of results A. Tables are available that show us for any particular F the probability (p) that an F of that size or larger might have occurred by chance. Reference to such tables shows us that results A could have occurred by chance less than five times in a thousand ($p < .005$) while results B could have occurred by chance very, very often. Frequently, in reading of the results of an experiment in the behavioral sciences, some statistic such as the F ratio will be reported along with some level of probability. The notation system is straightforward, such that $p \leq .10$ means that the chances are ten in a hundred or less that the obtained results could have occurred by chance; $p \leq .01$ means that the chances are one in a hundred or less that the obtained results could have occurred by chance.

Fully randomized designs are very common in the experimental behavioral sciences and, as might be expected, the most common sub-type is the simple situation of a single experimental group to be compared to a single control or comparison group. In such cases the F ratio we have described may also be employed although a more specialized statistic, t, is perhaps more commonly used. The simplest way to think of the t statistic is that it is the square root of the appropriate F ratio. As you might expect, there are tables available in which we can look up the p value associated with a t of any given size. As with F, the larger the t value the more unlikely that the variation between group means represented by the t value could have arisen by chance. The magnitude of t increases just as F does, not only as the dispersion between means or group averages increases but also as the dispersion of scores within groups decreases.

Suppose that we conducted an experiment not of four groups but of only two, such that we compared one group of children who were given vitamins with another group of children who were given nothing. Columns I and III of Table 6 give hypothetical results A and B. If we follow the calculations for F given earlier for just these two groups, we find $F = 9.38$ for results A, and $F = 1.04$ for results B. The corresponding t values are 3.06 ($p < .05$) and 1.02 ($p > .35$), suggesting that for results A, the five-point superiority of the vitamin group over the zero or "nothing" group means more than does the same degree of average difference found in results B. The reason, of course, stems from the fact that, within the conditions of results A, the scores are more tightly bunched than they are in the conditions of results B. Notice, for example, that the three vitamin group scores of results A (17, 15, 13) are all larger than are any of the three "nothing" group scores (12, 10, 8) while in results B the scores of the vitamin group (21, 15, 9) are more well scrambled with the results of the "nothing" group (16, 10, 4). Table

Table 7. Sample Listing of *t* Values

N–2	Probability Levels			
	.10	.05	.01	.005
4	2.13	2.78	4.60	5.60
8	1.86	2.31	3.36	3.83
16	1.75	2.12	2.92	3.25
40	1.68	2.02	2.70	2.97
∞	1.64	1.96	2.58	2.81

N denotes the total number of subjects in both groups or conditions. N–2 is called the degrees of freedom (*df*) for *t*.

7 provides a very abbreviated listing of *t* values required to reach any one of a number of levels of *p*, or, as they are usually referred to, levels of significance. Larger *t*s are associated with differences between means that are more "significantly different" from each other and which have, therefore, a lower level of *p*, or probability, that the differences might have arisen by chance. The left-hand column of Table 7 gives values of the quantity N-2, also known as the degrees of freedom (*df*) for *t*, which reflects the size of the experiment. The total number of research subjects involved in the comparison is the value N. The *t* test we computed earlier was based on two groups of three subjects each so that $N = 6$ and $N - 2 = 4$. With increases in the total number of subjects in the two samples, smaller values of *t* are required to reach the same level of significance.

Table 8 provides a sample listing of *F* values required to reach various levels of significance for fully randomized designs comparing two, three, or four groups. For the two-group comparison situation, it can be seen that *F* values are simply the squares of the analogous *t* values of Table 7.

TWO-DIMENSIONAL DESIGNS

These are research plans in which there is to be an assessment of the effects of two or more conditions each of which is itself assessed under two or more conditions. An example is essential, and we study again the hypothetical effects of nutrition on academic performance. Suppose that we change slightly the question we asked earlier about the differences among our four nutritional conditions. Let us ask several questions simultaneously:

Table 8.   Sample Listing of F Values

Groups	$N-a$	Probability Levels .10	.05	.01	.005
	4	4.54	7.71	21.20	31.33
	8	3.46	5.32	11.26	14.69
$a = 2$	16	3.05	4.49	8.53	10.58
	40	2.84	4.08	7.31	8.83
	∞	2.71	3.84	6.64	7.88
	4	4.32	6.94	18.00	26.28
	8	3.11	4.46	8.65	11.04
$a = 3$	16	2.67	3.63	6.23	7.51
	40	2.44	3.23	5.18	6.07
	∞	2.30	2.99	4.60	5.30
	4	4.19	6.59	16.69	24.26
	8	2.92	4.07	7.59	9.60
$a = 4$	16	2.46	3.24	5.29	6.30
	40	2.23	2.84	4.31	4.98
	∞	2.08	2.60	3.78	4.28

N = total number of subjects in all groups combined. $N-a$ is called the degrees of freedom (df) of the denominator of F.

a = number of groups being compared; ($a-1$) is called the degrees of freedom (df) of the numerator of F.

  1.   What is the effect on academic performance of daily milk?
  2.   What is the effect on academic performance of daily vitamins?
  3.   What is the effect on academic performance of both milk and vitamins?
  4.   Is the effect of vitamins different when milk is also given compared to when milk is not given?
  5.   Is the effect of milk different when vitamins are also given compared to when vitamins are not given?

All these questions can be answered by employing a two-dimensional design of the kind illustrated in Table 9.

The numerical values of Table 9 are the same as those of results A of Table 4. Subjects 1, 5, and 9 were randomly assigned to the no milk, no vitamins condition, subjects 2, 6, and 10 to the milk but no vitamins group, subjects 3, 7, and 11 to the vitamins but no milk group, and subjects 4, 8, and 12 to the milk-and-vitamins group. In the earlier example these last subjects had been assigned to the hot lunch condition, but for this example they were assigned to the milk-plus-vitamins condition.

Table 9.   Some Hypothetical Effects of Nutrition on Academic
Performance: Two-Dimensional Design

Treatment Conditions	No Milk	Milk	
No vitamins	$S_1 = 8$ $S_5 = 10$ $S_9 = 12$	$S_2 = 10$ $S_6 = 12$ $S_{10} = 14$	
	Sum = 30	Sum = 36	Row sum = 66
	Mean = 10	Mean = 12	Row mean = 11
Vitamins	$S_3 = 13$ $S_7 = 15$ $S_{11} = 17$	$S_4 = 17$ $S_8 = 19$ $S_{12} = 21$	
	Sum = 45	Sum = 57	Row sum = 102
	Mean = 15	Mean = 19	Row mean = 17
	Column sum = 75	Column sum = 93	Grand sum = 168
	Column mean = 12.5	Column mean = 15.5	Grand mean = 14

What have we gained by arraying our groups or conditions in two
dimensions (milk $\times$ vitamins) rather than in just the one dimension
comparing all four conditions? One advantage is that more of the subjects available for the experiment are able to contribute to the major
comparisons of the experiment (milk versus no milk; vitamins versus no
vitamins). Thus, half of all the subjects of the experiment are in the milk
conditions instead of the quarter of all subjects that would be in the milk
condition in a one-dimensional experiment. This half of the subjects can
be compared to the remaining half of the subjects who received no milk
so that all the subjects of the experiment shed light on the question of
the effect of milk. The effect of milk is assessed in Table 9 by a comparison of the milk and no milk averages. At the same time that all
subjects are providing information on the milk comparison, they are
also contributing information on the effects of vitamins. The effect of
vitamins is assessed in Table 9 by a comparison of the vitamin and
no-vitamin averages. That all subjects serve double duty is one of the
great advantages of two-dimensional designs. Each subject helps us to
learn about the effect of columns while at the same time teaching us
about the effect of rows.

Another advantage of the two-dimensional designs is that we can learn from them whether the effects of one of our dimensions, or factors, is much the same for each of the two or more conditions of the other factor. Looking at the means of the four conditions in Table 9 shows that there is a two-unit effect (12 minus 10 equals 2) of milk when no vitamins are given but a four-unit effect ($19 - 15 = 4$) of milk when vitamins are given. Similarly, there is a five-unit effect ($15 - 10 = 5$) of vitamins when no milk is given but a seven-unit effect ($19 - 12 = 7$) of vitamins when milk is given. These differences between differences are termed interaction effects, and their probability of having occurred by chance can be evaluated by the methods of the analysis of variance referred to earlier. For any given interaction effect, we judge its statistical significance by relating the magnitude of the effect to the magnitude of the variation within the conditions or cells of the experiment.

Table 10 shows a typical summary of an analysis of variance based, in this case, on the data of Table 9. We find in Table 10 two familiar entries, lines 1 and 5. Line 1 shows the variation among the four cell means that we had computed earlier. We recall the computations of line 1 as follows:

$$\frac{(30)^2/3 + (36)^2/3 + \cdots + (57)^2/3 - (168)^2/12}{4 - 1} = \frac{138}{3}$$

$$= \frac{\text{(sum of squares)}}{\text{(degrees of freedom, } df)} = \text{mean square} = 46$$

Line 5 shows the variation among the individual subjects within the four conditions of the experiment with computations as follows:

$$\frac{(8)^2 + (10)^2 + \cdots + (21)^2 - (30)^2/3 - (36)^2/3 - \cdots - (57)^2/3}{12 - 4} = \frac{32}{8}$$

$$= \frac{\text{(sum of squares)}}{\text{(degrees of freedom, } df)} = \text{mean square} = 4.$$

The last entry of line 1 shows the ratio of the mean square between the groups to the mean square within the groups. This ratio, the F ratio,

Table 10. Analysis of Variance of a Two-Dimensional Design

Source of Variation	Sum of Squares	df	Mean Squares	F
1. Between conditions	138	3	46	11.50
2. Milk	27	1	27	6.75
3. Vitamins	108	1	108	27.00
4. Milk × vitamins	3	1	3	0.75
5. Within conditions	32	8	4	—

was 11.50 as we recall from our earlier example. Reference to Table 8 showed us that an F of that magnitude is likely to occur very rarely unless there are real differences among the means of the four conditions.

So far we have had only a review of what was learned earlier. What we want to do now is to see the difference between the analysis of a one-dimensional design and a two-dimensional design. What we shall do is to subdivide the between-groups variation into the three components found in lines 2, 3, and 4 of Table 10. These three sources of variation are referred to as (a) the main effect of milk, (b) the main effect of vitamins, and (c) the interaction effect of milk and vitamins.

The variation associated with each of these three effects can be compared to the variation within conditions so that we can compute an F ratio for each that will permit inferences about the likelihood that effects of the obtained magnitude might have occurred by chance. The denominator for all three F ratios is the same: the mean square for within conditions. The numerators for the three F ratios are as follows:

1.   Mean square for main effect of milk (columns):

$$\frac{(T_{c_1})^2/n_{c_1} + (T_{c_2})^2/n_{c_2} + \cdots + (T_{c_c})^2/n_{c_c} - (\text{Total})^2/N}{a_c - 1}$$

$$= \frac{(\text{sum of squares})}{(\text{degrees of freedom, } df)} = \text{mean square}$$

where

T_{c_1} = the sum of the scores of the first column
T_{c_2} = the sum of the scores of the second column
T_{c_c} = the sum of the scores of the cth or last column
n_{c_1} = the number of scores of the first column
n_{c_2} = the number of scores of the second column
n_{c_c} = the number of scores of the cth or last column
Total = the sum of the scores added over all columns
a_c = the number of columns in the experiment

2.   Mean square for main effect of vitamins (rows):

$$\frac{(T_{r_1})^2/n_{r_1} + (T_{r_2})^2/n_{r_2} + \cdots + (T_{r_r})^2/n_{r_r} - (\text{Total})^2/N}{a_r - 1}$$

$$= \frac{(\text{sum of squares})}{(\text{degrees of freedom, } df)} = \text{mean square}$$

where

T_{r_1} = the sum of the scores of the first row
T_{r_2} = the sum of the scores of the second row
T_{r_r} = the sum of the scores of the rth or last row

$$n_{r_1} = \text{the number of scores of the first row}$$
$$n_{r_2} = \text{the number of scores of the second row}$$
$$n_{r_r} = \text{the number of scores of the } r^{\text{th}} \text{ or last row}$$
$$\text{Total} = \text{the sum of the scores added over all rows}$$
$$a_r = \text{the number of rows in the experiment}$$

3. Mean square for interaction of rows and columns:

$$\frac{(T_1{}^2/n_1 + T_2{}^2/n_2 + \cdots + T_a{}^2/n_a - (\text{Total})^2/N - \begin{smallmatrix}\text{(sum of}\\\text{squares}\\\text{for rows)}\end{smallmatrix} - \begin{smallmatrix}\text{(sum of}\\\text{squares for}\\\text{columns)}\end{smallmatrix}}{(a_c - 1)(a_r - 1)}$$

where

$$T_1 = \text{the sum of the scores of the first group or cell}$$
$$T_2 = \text{the sum of the scores of the second group or cell}$$
$$T_a = \text{the sum of the scores of the } a^{\text{th}} \text{ or last group or cell}$$
$$n_1 = \text{the number of scores of the first group or cell}$$
$$n_2 = \text{the number of scores of the second group or cell}$$
$$n_a = \text{the number of scores of the } a^{\text{th}} \text{ or last group or cell}$$
$$N = \text{the number of scores added over all groups or cells}$$
$$\text{Total} = \text{the sum of the scores added over all groups or cells}$$
$$a = \text{the number of groups or cells} = (a_c \times a_r)$$

(A restriction on the computational formulas given for the two-dimensional design is that the number of scores in each of the cells or conditions must be proportional from column to column and from row to row.)

For the data of Table 9, the mean square for the effect of milk is:

$$\frac{(75)^2/6 + (93)^2/6 - (168)^2/12}{2 - 1} = \frac{27}{1} = 27$$

The main effect of vitamins has an associated mean square of:

$$\frac{(66)^2/6 + (102)^2/6 - (168)^2/12}{2 - 1} = \frac{108}{1} = 108$$

The interaction mean square is:

$$\frac{(30)^2/3 + (36)^2/3 + \cdots + (57)^2/3 - (168)^2/12 - 27 - 108}{(2 - 1)\ (2 - 1)} = \frac{3}{1} = 3$$

The mean squares computed above are found in Table 10 along with the F ratios formed by dividing each by the mean square for within conditions. Reference to Table 8 (for $a = 2$, since only two conditions are being compared at a time) tells us that the F of 6.75 for the effect of milk could have occurred by chance less than five times in a hundred ($p < .05$). The F of 27.00 for the effect of vitamins could have occurred by

Table 11.   Reading Achievement in the Palardy Study

	Boys	Girls
Equal expectations for boys and girls	96.5	96.2
Lower expectation for boys than for girls	89.2	96.7

chance even less often ($p < .005$). The F for interaction, however, is so small that it could easily have arisen by chance. What we have learned from the subdivision of the between groups variation into the three components is that both milk and vitamins have a beneficial effect with more of the effect attributable to vitamins that to milk.

In our illustration the interaction was not significant, but we should note that often in behavioral research significant interactions are obtained. A recent example is that of Palardy (1969), who studied teachers' expectations for their pupils' success in learning to read. He found two groups of teachers, one in which boys were expected to do as well as girls and one in which boys were expected not to do as well as girls. Table 11 shows that there was no difference in the reading achievement of boys and girls taught by teachers who expected no difference but that boys did not do as well as girls in the classrooms of teachers who expected that boys would not do as well as girls.

TREATMENTS BY SUBJECTS

This third basic research plan can be seen as a special case of a two-dimensional design in which a number of experimental (or control) treatments are applied to each of a number of subjects. One dimension is the main effect of the treatments while the other dimension is the array of subjects. Because there is only a single score for each subject entered for each condition, there can be no estimate of within condition variation, but an F test of the main effect of treatments is often still possible, the mean square for treatments being divided by the mean square for the treatments $\times$ subjects interaction. Table 12 illustrates this design for our four familiar treatment conditions each of which has been applied, a month at a time, for example, to each of three different subjects. The analysis of variance is presented at the bottom of Table 12.

A great many other experimental designs are often found to be of value in behavioral research. Many of them, however, are related to the designs presented here so that an understanding of these three should make other designs more comprehensible on an intuitive level.

Table 12. Some Hypothetical Effects of Nutrition on Performance: Treatments-By-Subjects Design

	Treatment Conditions				
	Cond. I Zero	Cond. II Milk	Cond. III Vitamins	Cond. IV Hot Lunch	Totals
Subject 1	8	12	15	21	56
Subject 2	10	14	17	19	60
Subject 3	12	10	13	17	52
Sums	30	36	45	57	168
Means	10	12	15	19	14

Source	Sum of Squares	df	Mean Squares	F
Treatments	138	3	46	11.50
Subjects	8	2	4	—
Treatments $\times$ subjects	24	6	4	—

chapter five

other tests and measures of relationship

In the three experimental designs just summarized, the relationship between the independent variables and the dependent variables was expressed in terms of the F ratio of the analysis of variance. For any given sample size, the larger the F, the greater the relationship is between the independent variable (or variables) and the dependent variable and also the less likely that the relationship might have occurred by chance. There are a great many other tests and measures of relationship that are all related to one another in various ways.

PEARSON CORRELATION COEFFICIENT

The Pearson correlation coefficient, symbolized by r, is an index of the strength of relationship. It can take on values from -1.00 through zero to $+1.00$. A correlation near zero means that the two variables in question are relatively unrelated. A correlation near $+1.00$ means that the greater the value or score on one variable, the greater the value or score on the other variable. A correlation near -1.00 means that the greater the score on one variable, the lower the score on the other variable. From the point of view of estimating a score on one variable from one's knowledge of a score on the other variable, it makes no difference whether the correlation is very close to $+1.00$ or to -1.00; both correlations would predict equally well.

A useful characteristic of the Pearson r is that when squared and multiplied by 100 it states the percentage of variation in one variable estimable from the other. Thus, an r of ±1.00 means that 100 percent of the variation in one variable can be accounted for on the basis of knowledge of the other variable. Similarly, for an r of .80, 64 percent of the variation in variable Y can be accounted for by variable X; and for rs of .50 and .30, the percentages of accounted for variation would be 25% and 9%, respectively.

Actually, it is also possible to express for an F ratio the percentage of variation in the dependent variable that can be accounted for on the basis of knowledge of the independent variable. The procedure for this transformation of F to an estimate of the percentage of variance accounted for requires us to take into account the df of the numerator of F as well as the df of the denominator. We recall that the numerator df is related to the number of groups or conditions being compared by means of F, while the denominator df is related to the total number of subjects of the experiment. The formula for determining the percentage of variation accounted for (P) is

$$P = \frac{(F)\,(df \text{ numerator})}{(F)\,(df \text{ numerator}) + (df \text{ denominator})}$$

Knowing this relationship we can also calculate P when we have employed a t test instead of an F test. We need only recall that t is related to F such that $t^2 = F$. Therefore, we need only square our t and then treat it as an F with only a single df in the numerator. The df for the denominator will be N-2 or the total number of subjects less 2. In sum,

$$P = \frac{t^2}{t^2 + N - 2}$$

or, equivalently

$$P = \frac{F}{F + df \text{ denominator}}$$

Examination of the formulas given shows that a greater proportion of variance will be accounted for by ts or Fs of any given value that are based on smaller numbers of subjects within each of the conditions of the experiment.

One workaday use for the correlation coefficient is to establish whether two observers who are coding natural-setting behavior are in good agreement with one another, or what is called intercoder reliability. If two observers are to code the warmth of classroom teachers and they cannot agree on what constitutes "warmth," then the resulting ratings given to teachers on the variable of warmth cannot be very useful. The higher the correlation, the more are our observers in agreement on what constitutes teachers' warmth. Table 13 shows some hypothetical ratings in such a check on observer reliability. The two observers, X and Y, rated

Table 13.   Some Hypothetical Ratings of Teachers'
Warmth by Two Observers: Pearson *r*

Teachers Rated	Observer X	Observer Y	X²	Y²	XY
a	5	4	25	16	20
b	5	3	25	9	15
c	4	5	16	25	20
d	4	4	16	16	16
e	4	3	16	9	12
f	3	3	9	9	9
g	3	1	9	1	3
h	2	2	4	4	4
i	1	2	1	4	2
N = 9	ΣX = 31	ΣY = 27	ΣX² = 121	ΣY² = 93	ΣXY = 101

nine teachers on warmth in the classroom on a scale that ranged from a score of 5 for maximum warmth to 1 for minimum warmth.

The computational formula for the Pearson correlation coefficient is:

$$r = \frac{N(\Sigma XY) - (\Sigma X)(\Sigma Y)}{\sqrt{[N(\Sigma X^2) - (\Sigma X)^2][N(\Sigma Y^2) - (\Sigma Y)^2]}}$$

where

N = number of X and Y pairs of ratings
X = any rating by observer X
Y = any rating by observer Y
Σ = summation sign, a mathematical symbol directing us to obtain the sum of a set of values

Substituting in this formula the values from Table 13 gives the following:

$$r = \frac{9(101) - (31)(27)}{\sqrt{[9(121) - (31)^2][9(93) - (27)^2]}}$$
$$= \frac{909 - 837}{\sqrt{(128)(108)}}$$
$$= \frac{72}{117.58}$$
$$= .61$$

Hence, for these two observers the correlation between their ratings was +.61, a value that, while not very close to 1.00, nevertheless is adequate for such global ratings of real-life behavior.

For any particular value of r we can assess the statistical significance, or probability, that an r of that size might have occurred by chance. We solve for t in the following:

$$t = \frac{r\sqrt{N-2}}{\sqrt{1-r^2}}$$

and then look up the p value associated with t in Table 7. Of course, how to interpret the size of a correlation coefficient will depend on the way we propose to use it as well as on its statistical significance. A Pearson r of .40 might be satisfactorily high for some purposes but too low for others. In the case of intercoder reliability, it may appear rather low, and a correlation coefficient of .61 would certainly be more impressive by comparison. However, in the case of what is called validity, a correlation of .40 could be quite satisfactory (Cohen, 1969).

The Case of Validity—and More on Reliability

Validity refers to the degree to which something does what it purports to do. Reliability refers to the degree to which that something does its job consistently. Applying these concepts in the area of psychological testing, for instance, can help us to evaluate the usefulness of a measuring instrument. Before turning to a consideration of the concept of validity we want to note that there is more than one procedure for estimating reliability in psychological test construction.

There are three very useful methods of evaluating reliability in psychological testing. They all use a correlation coefficient (not always the Pearson, however) but on quite different data to give information on quite different questions. One is the test-retest method, which applies the correlation coefficient to data from the same test but obtained at different times. The test is administered twice to the same group of people, and the aim is to determine how consistently they responded. Second is the equivalent-forms method, which applies the correlation coefficient to data from comparable forms of the same test. Both forms are administered to the same group of people, and the aim is to determine whether the two forms measure the same thing. Third is the split-half method, which applies the correlation coefficient to comparable halves of the same test. The test is split in two, and both parts are administered to the same group of people, the aim in this instance being to determine if the test is internally consistent.

In contrast to reliability (which tells how consistently something measures whatever it measures), validity tells us whether that "something" actually measures what it claims to measure. In order to assess the validity of a psychological test we would need some good criteria against which to check the test's accuracy. For example, if we were developing a test of college aptitude we might employ as our criterion the successful completion of the first year of college or maybe grade-point average after each year of college. If we were developing a test to measure anxiety, we might use as our criterion the pooled judgments of a group of highly trained clinicians who have rated each person to whom we administered the test. In the validation of our observations we try to select the most sensible and meaningful criterion for the purpose at hand. We must also be concerned about the reliability of the criterion. Grade-point average tends to be a fairly reliable criterion, whereas clinicians' judgments about complex behavior may be a less reliable criterion. However, reliability can be increased by adding more data readings or greater numbers of judgments—in the latter instance above, by adding more clinicians to the group whose pooled judgments will serve as our criterion (Rosenthal, 1973a).

Sometimes we must even be concerned about the validity of the criterion itself. Suppose that we want to develop a short test of anxiety that will predict the scores on a longer test of anxiety. The longer test serves as our criterion, and the new short test may be relatively quite valid with respect to the longer test. However, the longer test may itself be of dubious validity with respect to some other criterion, say clinicians' judgments. Sometimes, then, criteria must be evaluated with respect to other criteria, and there are no firm rules (beyond the consensus of the researchers in an area of inquiry) as to what shall constitute an ultimate criterion.

Three important kinds of validity can be distinguished by their location in time. These are predictive validity, concurrent validity, and postdictive validity.

When the criterion is in the future, we speak of predictive validity. Tests of college aptitude are normally assessed for predictive validity since the criteria of graduation and grade-point average are in the future with respect to the predictive tests. The aptitude test scores are saved until the future criterion data become available and are then correlated with them, the resulting correlation coefficient serving as a statement of predictive validity.

When the criterion is in the present, we speak of concurrent validity. Clinical diagnostic tests are normally assessed for concurrent validity since the criterion of the patients' true diagnostic status is in the present with respect to the tests we are trying to validate. Shorter forms of longer tests are often evaluated with respect to their concurrent validity using the longer test as the criterion. It could reasonably be argued in such cases that it is not validity but reliability that is being assessed. Indeed, while reliability and validity are conceptually distinguishable, it is sometimes difficult to separate them in practice.

When the criterion is in the past, we speak of postdictive validity. Observations in forensic psychiatry are normally assessed for postdictive validity since the criterion of criminal or psychopathological behavior is in the past with respect to the observations being validated. Thus, a court may want a determination of whether a person was capable of a given, unusual act, whether he knew at the time that it was "right" or "wrong," and whether he was capable of controlling his actions.

Predictive, concurrent, and postdictive validities can all be expressed by a single correlation coefficient between the tests (or observations) being assessed for validity and the data based on a single criterion. There is another type of validity in which only a single criterion is employed: content validity. The criterion for the assessment of content validity is an exhaustive listing of all the material that the observations to be validated were designed to sample. The common use of content validation is in the assessment of tests of achievement, or content mastery. A test is regarded as more content valid the more it covers adequately the facts, ideas, and concepts that define the material of the area, course, or unit of study. While the other forms of validity considered so far can be expressed by a correlation coefficient between the tests being validated and a criterion, content validity is usually expressed as a global, nonquantitative judgment or in terms of the adequacy of sampling of the contents to be covered.

More sophisticated views of the validation of tests, or of observations generally, require that we be sensitive not only to the correlation between our measures and some appropriate criterion but also to the correlation between our measures and some inappropriate criterion. Suppose we developed a measure of adjustment and find that it correlates .60 with our criterion of the pooled judgment of expert clinicians. That would be an attractive outcome of a concurrent validation effort. Suppose further, however, that we administer a test of intelligence to all of our subjects and find that the correlation between our adjustment scores and intelligence is also .60. Would our new test be a reasonably valid test of adjustment, of intelligence, of both, or of neither? That question is difficult to answer, but we could not claim on the basis of these results to understand our new test very well. It was not intended, after all, to be a measure of intelligence. In short, our test has good concurrent validity but poor differential validity. It does not correlate differentially with criteria for different types of observation.

Many sets of observations and tests in the behavioral sciences are designed to measure fundamental constructs of theoretical importance. In measuring anxiety or intelligence we are interested not simply in predicting or postdicting some other variable, the criterion, but also in getting at the underlying construct. Just as no set of observations we wish to validate can be regarded as *the* measure of the construct, no single criterion can be regarded as *the* definition of the construct. Construct validation requires the employment of multiple criteria and has, as its aim, as much the validation of the underlying construct as of the test designed to measure the construct. Construct validation may require the employment of all the other types of validity we have discussed. The level of construct validation of a set of observations is generally expressed in prose rather than in single correlation coefficients or even in differences between two correlation coefficients. That is because the level of construct validation depends on virtually all we know at any one time about our test, or set of observations, as well as all we know about the construct that our measures are designed to tap.

Cross-Lagged Data

The interpretation and comparison of correlation coefficients is also the basis of another useful inquiry procedure in behavioral science, in this case a means of assessing causality via cross-lagged data analyses.

Suppose we were interested in the relationship between television violence and aggression, and we were given data on the TV viewing habits of a representative sample of children and also peer ratings of their aggressiveness by posing the question to each, "Who started fights over nothing?" If the correlation coefficient was a positive value, this would tell us that the children who watched more violent TV were also the more aggressive. If it were a negative value, this would tell us that the children who watched more violent TV were less aggressive. Neither correlation could, by itself, reveal whether TV viewing and aggressivity were linked in a causal fashion. Indeed, there are at least four rival hypotheses that are plausible: (a) aggression is the independent variable and the preference for violent TV is the dependent variable, (b) aggression is the dependent variable and the preference for TV violence is the independent variable, (c) both are independent variables, or (d) both are dependent variables and some other variable is their common cause.

One way to begin to unravel the puzzle is to look at the correlations across the two variables over a period of time, or what is called a cross-lagged analysis (Rozelle and Campbell, 1969). By examining the temporal cross correlations of the variables, it is possible to rule out some of the rival hypotheses and thus narrow the field down a little.

An illustration of the procedure on this very issue occurs in a

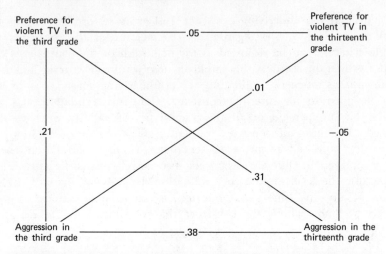

FIGURE 2. Correlations between a preference for violent television and peer-rated aggression for 211 boys over a 10-year lag. (After Eron, Huesmann, Lefkowitz, & Walder, 1972).

recent study by Eron, Huesmann, Lefkowitz, and Walder (1972), some of the results of which are shown in Figure 2. The correlations given on the diagonals, .01 and .31, are the cross-lagged analyses, and the other correlations describe the strength of relationship of all the other possible combinations of the variables.

Thus, we find a small but definite positive relationship between the preference for violent TV and aggression among third-graders ($r = .21$), but a miniscule, negative relationship between the same variables when the students were in high school (called the thirteenth-grade period). If there is a cause-and-effect relationship here—the direction of which we cannot tell from these two correlations alone—it appears to be one that was established in childhood and not in adolescence, judging from the comparative size of the two correlations. Indeed, there is little relationship between these students' viewing habits in childhood and their TV preferences as adolescents ($r = .05$), although the correlation of .38 for aggressivity may imply a persistent pattern of aggressive behavior once learned.

Turning now to the cross-lagged correlations, it should be possible to hypothesize the direction of any causal relationship here merely by comparing the location and size of these two correlations. We know that there was a ten-year difference between the measures on the left and those on the right, the one set of measures representing data collected from children when they were in the third grade and the other, after the children had graduated from high school. We want to know which was the likely independent variable—exposure to TV violence or actual aggressive behaviors. The negligible cross-lagged correlation of .01 between aggression in the third grade and preference for violent TV in the thirteenth grade would seem to rule out the idea that aggressiveness per se was a determinant of the children's subsequent TV viewing habits. Squaring the correlation tells us that none of the variation in the high schoolers' preferences for violent TV can be predicted from their aggressive behavior when children. By contrast, the positive relationship of .31 between preferences for violent TV in the third grade and aggression in the thirteenth grade implies that the students could have learned some of their later aggressive behaviors from what they saw on television as children. Squaring this correlation tells us that there must also be other significant variables operating, for less than 10 percent of the variation in the high schoolers' aggressiveness can be accounted for by their childhood preferences for violent TV. Still, the relationship is a promising one and would lead the investigators to gather additional data bearing on the postulated causal association. By comparing their findings with other relevant data, this would further enable them to assess the inferred relationship (cf. Huesmann, Eron, Lefkowitz, and Walder, 1973). The actual interpretation of the present results is complicated by the very low retest reliability of one of the variables (preference for violent TV, $r = .05$), which is a plausible contributor to the low cross-lagged correlation of .01 (Kenny, 1972).

This interesting study also illustrates a variation of nonexperimental observation in which causal inferences can be cautiously made on the basis of simple correlations but which are cross lagged. This particular type of investigation, which examines the same sample of subjects over a long period of time, is known as longitudinal research. While it can be expensive to do, and is obviously time consuming, the longitudinal study is an excellent way of observing how small effects, sometimes imperceptible at a given moment, can grow into dramatic, explicit form. The longitudinal research paradigm might be compared to a filmstrip where the frames correspond to consecutive observations of behavior—a, b, c, and so forth, through frame z. Let us say, that our aim is to predict the behavior or interplay of events in frame z. We can see intuitively that the likelihood of the prediction being accurate could depend on the number of preceding frames neighboring z that contained reliable observations of the occurrence in question. Whether the final frame is a picture of people interacting or one of events on a larger social scale, the longitudinal approach could be a very useful method to employ.

CHI SQUARE

In our discussion of the correlation coefficient (r) we noted that it could be viewed quite directly as a measure of the degree of relationship between two variables. Indeed, we had only to square r to obtain the proportion of variance of one of the variables estimable from a knowledge of the other variable. However, when the number of pairs of scores on which r is based is small, a very large r may not differ significantly from chance. In that case we would be forced to say that although there was a strong relationship between our two variables, relationships that strong could occur quite often by chance even if the true correlation between our variables were zero. For that reason we would like to know for any r not only its size but also its probability of having occurred by chance. We therefore gave a formula for testing this probability by means of a t test.

While r tells us immediately how "big" a relationship there is between variables but not how unlikely it is to have occurred by chance, F and t tell us immediately how unlikely it is that a given relationship could have occurred by chance but not how "big" the relationship is. However, by taking a simple additional step, described earlier, we can compute the size of the relationship that a large F or t have convinced us is unlikely to have occurred by chance. Thus, r gives us size of relationship and permits us further to assess statistical significance while F and t give us statistical significance and permit us further to assess size of relationship.

The statistic we discuss in this section is the chi square, symbolized as χ^2. It is a statistic that, like F and t, tells us how unlikely it is that the relationship investigated could have occurred by chance, but, like F and t, does not tell us immediately about the strength of the relationship between the variables. Just as in the case of F and t, any given value of χ^2 will be associated with a stronger degree of relationship when it is based on a smaller number of subjects. To put it another way, a relationship must be quite strong to result in a large χ^2 (or F, or t) with only a small number of subjects.

Chi square does its job of testing the relationship between two variables by assessing the discrepancy between a theoretically expected and an obtained frequency. It differs from the other tests of association we have examined in that it can be used for dependent variables that are not scored or scaled. In all the earlier examples, subjects' responses were recorded as scores such that some could be regarded as so many units greater or less than other scores. The χ^2 statistic allows us to deal with categories of response that are not so easily ordered, scaled, or scored.

Table 14. Some Hypothetical Party Memberships and Preferences for Political Candidates: Chi Square

		Candidates	Party I	Party II	Party III	Row Totals
A	Obtained frequencies	Smith	15	14	7	36
		Jones	14	3	10	27
		Brown	11	13	3	27
		Column totals	40	30	20	90
B	Expected frequencies	Smith	16	12	8	36
		Jones	12	9	6	27
		Brown	12	9	6	27
		Column totals	40	30	20	90
C	$\dfrac{(A\text{-}B)^2}{B}$	Smith	.06	.33	.12	.51
		Jones	.33	4.00	2.67	7.00
		Brown	.08	1.78	1.50	3.36
		Column totals	.47	6.11	4.29	10.87

Suppose, for example, that we wanted to learn whether there was any association between subjects' membership in one of several political parties and their preference for any one of several alternative candidates for political office. Membership in a political party is thought of as the independent variable while the preference for Smith, Brown, or Jones is the dependent variable as shown in section A of Table 14. Each member of the sample of subjects asked to state their preference falls into one and only one of the nine possible cells. The frequencies in the cell refer to the number of people in that column (party) who prefer the particular candidate listed in that row. Thus, there are 14 members of the sample who affiliated with Party II and who prefer candidate Smith, while 11 members of Party I prefer Brown, etc.

In order to compute χ^2 we must first determine for each cell of the table the number of expected entries. This expected frequency is computed for each cell by multiplying the column total by the row total for that row and that column that intersect in the cell in question, then dividing this quantity by the grand total number of entries. The upper left cell of section A in Table 14 is at the intersection of column I and Smith's row. The appropriate totals multiplied together and divided by the grand total are thus: (40) (36)/90 = 16. The expected frequency for the cell formed at the intersection of column III and

Table 15.   Sample Listing of χ^2 Values

(R–1) (C–1)	Probability Levels			
	.10	.05	.01	.005
1	2.71	3.84	6.63	7.88
2	4.61	5.99	9.21	10.60
4	7.78	9.49	13.28	14.86
8	13.36	15.51	20.09	21.96
24	33.20	36.42	42.98	45.56

$R =$ number of rows.
$C =$ number of columns.
$(R–1)$ $(C–1)$ is called the degrees of freedom (df) of the chi square.

Brown's row is: (20) (27)/90 = 6. Section B of Table 14 gives all the expected frequencies computed in this way. Section C of Table 14 gives for each cell the square of the difference between the obtained and expected frequency divided by the expected frequency. For just the first row, these values are: $(15\text{-}16)^2/16$, $(14\text{-}12)^2/12$, $(7\text{-}8)^2/8 = .06$, .33, and .12. The total of all these values is the χ^2, which in this case is 10.87.

The larger the χ^2, the less likely it is that the obtained frequencies differ only by chance from the expected frequencies. Table 15 gives a sample listing of χ^2 values for each of a number of p values. To find the appropriate line on which to enter the table, we multiply the number of rows less one (3 minus 1) times the number of columns less one (3 minus 1) to obtain the value 4. The number obtained by multiplying (number of rows minus one, or $R - 1$) by (number of columns minus one, or $C - 1$) is called the degrees of freedom (df) of the chi square. Our obtained value of χ^2 was 10.87, which falls between the .05 and .01 levels of statistical significance. There are, then, less than five chances in a hundred that a χ^2 so large could have occurred by chance.

When there are many cells in a χ^2 table, a statistically significant χ^2 may be difficult to interpret. The construction of an intermediate table such as that of section C in Table 14 can be of help. The entries of that section show which of the cells contributed most to the overall large χ^2. A large cell entry in this table of $(A\text{-}B)^2/B$ values indicates that the cell in question is surprising to us, or unexpected, given the magnitude of the row and column totals which are affected by that cell. In Table 14 the largest value of section C suggests that for Party II, surprisingly few members voted for Jones while the second largest value of section C suggests that for Party III, surprisingly many members voted for Jones.

Partitioning Chi Square Tables

In a large table of χ^2 it is sometimes desirable, when the overall χ^2 is interestingly large, to compute some additional χ^2s based on portions of the overall table. Either a prior theory or the nature of the obtained results can serve to guide our judgment as to which additional χ^2s to compute. Such a procedure, which enables one to draw inferences about interactions when there are more than two rows and two columns of data, is the partitioning method (Castellan, 1965; Bresnahan and Shapiro, 1966). This is a way of subdividing a large chi square table into component tables that can be more easily interpreted in a logical sequence. The number and size of the component tables are guided by a few simple rules. To illustrate the approach, we borrow from Castellan's (1965) instructive paper on this subject.

Table 16 presents his hypothetical data in a 2×4 (2 rows and 4 columns) table. It states that we have information on some variable, Y, and that some people are high Ys and others are low Ys. Thus, Table 16 shows that 21 out of a sample of 35 rural Indians are high Ys, that 8 local Indians scored high and 3 scored low, and so on. Using the method of computing chi square just described would give a chi square value of 14.03 for Table 16. By referring to Table 15 for $(R - 1 = 1)$ times $(C - 1 = 3)$, or between the values of 2 and 4 in that left-hand column, we learn that this chi square value of 14.03 must be significant beyond the .01 level, which can be expressed as $p < .01$. In fact, if you care to interpolate the chi square value to get a more precise estimate of probability, you will discover that it has a significance probability of $p < .005$, which indicates a very large chi square indeed. What this highly significant chi square tells us is that, somewhere in these data, the observed proportions do not match

Table 16. Some Hypothetical Data from Castellan (1965) to Illustrate the Partitioning of Tables

Variables	Rural Indian (RI)	Local Indian (LI)	Spanish (S)	Anglo (A)	Sum
High Y	21	8	24	13	66
Low Y	14	3	12	30	59
Sum	35	11	36	43	125

the corresponding theoretical proportions. However, it does not tell us just where those discrepancies occur; for this information, we need to partition the table. Because multiplying $R - 1$ times $C - 1$ gives us a value of 3 for a 2×4 table, we are permitted to obtain three partitions, or subdivisions. The particular subdivisions we choose will be guided by the kind of information sought, and a separate analysis will be computed on each of the three component tables to give us this information.

Suppose that the three partitions we selected allowed comparisons to be made for the following interactions:

1.   RI $\times$ LI: the rural Indian and local Indian comparison.
2.   (RI-LI) $\times$ S: the Indian-Spanish comparison.
3.   (RI-LI-S) $\times$ A: the nonAnglo-Anglo comparison.

Without going into the statistical calculations—which are routine and should be easy to follow if you study Castellan's paper with its sample analyses now that you are familiar with the logic of the chi square analysis—Table 17 shows these subdivisions of the original 2×4 table that correspond to the three interactions; it also provides a summary of his reported statistical results. We see that the chi squares for the rural Indian-local Indian comparison and for the Indian-Spanish comparison are both quite negligible and that their probabilities are thus appropriately shown as *ns*, or nonsignificant. For the third comparison, however, the chi square is very large, its probability significance exceeding the .005 level in Table 15. Hence, our partitioning of the data in Table 16 now enables us to state exactly where the significant interaction occurred, which was in the nonAnglo-Anglo comparison.

Standardizing the Margins

The principle of taking a fairly complex array of results and simplifying it by breaking it up into more manageable pieces is not restricted to chi square tables. We employed the same principle earlier in our discussion of a two-dimensional design. The first row of Table 10 gave the overall differences among the four conditions of the experiment on the effects of milk and vitamins. The resulting F ratio was large enough to tell us that there were differences among the four groups, but it could not tell us where the important differences were. It could not tell us, for example, whether milk made a difference, whether vitamins made a difference, or whether milk or vitamins made a bigger difference. The next three rows of Table 10 partitioned the overall differ-

Table 17. Component Tables Derived from Table 16 and
Summary of the Statistical Analyses

	Variables	Rural Indian	Local Indian
RI × LI	High Y	21	8
	Low Y	14	3

	Variables	Indian	Spanish
(RI–LI) × S	High Y	29	24
	Low Y	17	12

	Variables	non-Anglo	Anglo
(RI–LI–S) × A	High Y	53	13
	Low Y	29	30

Source	$(R-1)(C-1)^a$	χ^2	p
RI × LI	1	.54	ns
(RI–LI) × S	1	.10	ns
(RI–LI–S) × A	1	13.39	$p < .005$
Total	3	14.03	$p < .005$

$a(R-1)(C-1)$ = degrees of freedom of χ^2.

ences among the four groups into three very specific differences or
"contrasts." These contrasts or differences tested, in order, (a) the effects
of milk, (b) the effects of vitamins, and (c) the effects of having both
milk and vitamins or neither milk nor vitamins (compared to having
one or the other). Thus, whether applied to tables of frequencies as
in the chi square table or to analyses of variance as in the milk and
vitamins experiment, the principle of simplifying or partitioning the
data array into more manageable pieces, or contrasts, has great generality
and great utility.

One of the special problems of trying to understand the data of large
contingency tables (chi square tables) is that our eye is likely to be
fooled by the absolute magnitude of the frequencies displayed. Suppose
we were to ask of the data of Table 16 which group of subjects was
most overrepresented in the category "high Y." Our eye notes that the

rural Indian and Spanish groups have the greatest frequency of occurrence in that category, and we might erroneously conclude that one of these groups was most overrepresented in the high Y category. Our conclusion would be in error because we looked only into the table and not, at the same time, at the sums in the row and column margins. A look at those margins suggests that the rural Indian and Spanish groups should have larger frequencies in the high Y category than the local Indian group because there are more members of the former two samples than of the latter sample. In addition, there are slightly more subjects in general in the high Y category than in the low Y category. Taking all these margins into account simultaneously would show us that it was actually the local Indians who were most overrepresented in the high Y category.

In very large contingency tables, however, "taking the margins into account" becomes a very difficult matter without employing systematic aids to eye and mind. Fortunately, Frederic Mosteller (1968) has presented us with a systematic procedure for taking the margins into account called "standardizing the margins." The idea is to make all row margins equal at the same time making all column margins equal. For the data of Table 16 we begin by dividing each frequency in the table by its column margin or sum. That yields the following table:

Table 16a

	RI	LI	S	A	Sum
High Y	.600	.727	.667	.302	2.296
Low Y	.400	.273	.333	.698	1.704
Sum	1.000	1.000	1.000	1.000	4.000

Table 16a has equalized the column margins, but it has done nothing to equalize the row margins. To do so requires that we now divide each of the new values of Table 16a by its row margin or sum yielding the following table:

Table 16b

	RI	LI	S	A	Sum
High Y	.261	.317	.291	.132	1.001
Low Y	.235	.160	.195	.410	1.000
Sum	.496	.477	.486	.542	2.001

Table 16*b* has equalized the row margins, at least within rounding error, but now the column margins are no longer equal. By now we know what to do about that: simply divide each entry of Table 16*b* by its new column margin. That will equalize the column margins but make our new row margins unequal. We repeat, or "iterate", this procedure until further iterations no longer affect our margins. For the present data we formed five more tables of the type shown above but we present here only the final one:

Table 16c

	RI	LI	S	A	Sum
High *Y*	.517	.657	.589	.238	2.001
Low *Y*	.483	.343	.411	.762	1.999
Sum	1.000	1.000	1.000	1.000	4.000

Table 16*c* shows margins equalized within rounding error, and it allows us to interpret the table entries without worrying about the confusing effects of variations in margins. It shows that the local Indian group is overrepresented most in the high *Y* category while the Anglo group is overrepresented most in the low *Y* category.

There is one more step we can take to throw the results into still bolder relief: show the cell entries as deviations from the values we would expect if there were no differences whatever among the groups in their representation in the high *Y* or low *Y* categories. If, in fact, there were no such differences and given the margins of Table 16*c*, all the values in the table would be .500. In forming our final table we subtract this expected value of .500 from each entry of Table 16*c*:

Table 16d

	RI	LI	S	A	Sum
High *Y*	+.017	+.157	+.089	−.262	+.001
Low *Y*	−.017	−.157	−.089	+.262	−.001
Sum	.000	.000	.000	.000	.000

The interpretation of Table 16*d* is fairly direct and quite consistent with the χ^2 analysis shown in Table 17. The big difference is between the Anglos who are overrepresented very heavily in the low *Y* category and all other groups which are more modestly overrepresented in the high Y category. However, disregarding the fact that the sample sizes were sometimes too small to be very stable, we also raise some tentative questions about differences among the three groups overrepresented in the high Y group. The local Indians are substantially more overrepresented in the high Y category than are the rural Indians who are virtually not overrepresented at all. The Spanish group fell almost exactly midway between the two Indian groups in degree of overrepresentation in the high Y category. For the small sample sizes of the present study, the differences among these three groups are not significant statistically but with larger sample sizes, they might be. In any case, the purpose of the procedure of standardizing the margins is to highlight differences among groups whether these differences achieve statistical significance or not.

chapter six

problems of inference

OBSERVATIONAL REACTIVITY

When an engineer carefully takes the dimensions of a large piece of metal, we don't suppose that the act of measurement will have much of an effect on the metal. When a biologist observes the movements of a paramecium, we shouldn't expect that the paramecium will behave much differently when the scientist's eye is to the microscope than if he is looking away from it. However, one may be less sure of the risks of observational reactivity when primates are the object of study. Is the chimpanzee's behavior apt to be affected by his awareness of having captured the attentive interest of the behavioral scientist? With human subjects, the problem of observational reactivity is, of course, even more salient.

One researcher, Martin T. Orne, found this out in the course of a program of research on hypnosis when he tried to devise a set of dull, meaningless tasks that nonhypnotized control subjects would either refuse to do or would try for only a short time. One task was to add hundreds of thousands of two-digit numbers until the experimenter told them to stop. Five and a half hours after the subjects began, the experimenter gave up! Even when they were told to tear each work sheet into no less than 32 pieces before going on to the next, the subjects still persisted.

Orne's (1962) explanation for this unusually compliant behavior was that they were reacting to the fact that they were research subjects.

Feeling that they had a stake in the outcome of the scientist's observa-
ions of their behavior, they placed meaning in a meaningless chore.
Perhaps they thought that, no matter how trivial and inane the task
seemed to them, the researcher must certainly have an important scientific purpose that justified their work on the addition problems. They
may have rationalized that they were making a useful scientific contribution by acquiescing to the researcher's demands.

This motive of making a habit of being useful may not be an un-
common effect of observational reactivity in behavioral research. However, if some people are eager to play "good subject," others seem to
want to take the opposite role. The question of how to tease out this
behavior so as to draw valid inferences about the relationships being
studied has been an object of much concern in the behavioral sciences.

One way of conceptualizing this methodological problem is in terms
of what sociologists call role theory. This theoretical orientation derives from the dramaturgical analogy: it assumes that a large part of
human behavior is guided and constrained by the social prescriptions
and behavior of others. For the human research subject, it is recognized
that he, no less than other socialized human beings, must be sensitive
to the coercive demands of whatever propriety norms are operating. For
example, in laboratory experimentation in the behavioral sciences, the
object is to observe social processes in a precisely controlled standard
situation where one can manipulate some given independent variable
(or carefully interfere with some normally occurring naturalistic relationship) while holding other elements of the situation constant. To
be able to draw inferences from the research findings that are generaliz-
able to the analogous situation outside the laboratory requires that the
experimental conditions closely reflect the social processes under investigation. However, insofar as the research subjects are motivated in
a different way than they would be in the naturalistic situation and are
responding to artificial cues and conditions, it will be very difficult to
draw legitimate inferences which can be generalized to real life conditions.

By no means is the problem restricted to experimental research.
In survey and interview research, for example, the risks of observational
reactivity are also very high. The phrasing of a question may seem to
reveal presumptions as to its answers, and the good subject may be most
eager to fulfill the questioner's expectations (cf. Fillenbaum, 1968).
How can one deal with a problem that is perhaps inherent in human
behavioral research? To answer this question in a simple, practical way,
it will be instructive to examine the problem from a broader perspective
and to consider some of the main variables responsible for the biasing
effects of observational reactivity.

ROLE BEHAVIOR OF RESEARCH SUBJECTS

There is considerable evidence to suggest that, within the context of our Western culture, the role of research subject is probably well understood by the majority of normal adults who find their way into our subject pools (e.g., Epstein, Suedfeld, and Silverstein, 1973). In psychology, at least, most of them will be college undergraduates (Higbee and Wells, 1972; Schultz, 1969; Smart, 1966)—usually a cooperative and readily accessible population—prompting one authority to quip, "The existing science of human behavior is largely the science of the behavior of sophomores" (McNemar, 1946). What are the factors that can influence the role behaviors of such subjects and that may systematically bias the outcomes of the behavioral scientist's research efforts? Viewing the research setting as a social influence situation, a recent interpretation of subjects' role behaviors is based upon a five-step information-processing model (Rosnow and Aiken, 1973).

Step I is the origin of the research subject's role expectations. Subjects' ideas about what the researcher wants are a mixture of various hints in the procedure. Orne (1962) has coined the term "demand characteristics" to describe these hints, which are the totality of cues governing subjects' perceptions of their roles and of the researcher's hypotheses. Presumably the subject evaluates demand characteristics in the context of other information, such as the instructions, the setting, rumors about the purpose of the experiment, and especially his impressions of the experimenter. For example, one very potent source of demand characteristics is the subject's preconceptions and modeling behavior (Rosenthal, 1966, 1967, 1969). Modeling cues arise when the researcher projects his views onto the subject. Exactly why these effects should occur is unclear, although it appears that the emotional tone conveyed by the researcher can be a source of satisfaction or dissatisfaction for the subject and thus shape his behavior in much the same way that ordinary rewards and punishments can reinforce social behavior (cf. Jones and Cooper, 1971). How the subject processes these demand characteristics will depend on whatever other things are linked to these in his mind. However, in order to be processed, first the demand characteristics must be properly received.

Step 2 is receptivity. The scientific atmosphere of the research setting, how experienced the subject is in the ways of behavioral science, his perspicacity and intelligence—any of these factors could affect his facility at recognizing and interpreting demand characteristics. The typical research subject is an active, aware person who is probably quite interested in the project or he wouldn't be there in the first place. Because he wants to be helpful and at the same time to project a favorable image, he should be highly sensitive to whatever task orienting cues are operating in the situation. For example, Silverman (1968) did an attitude change experiment in which he varied one main aspect of the situation by having the teacher and the experimenter emphasize for the subjects that they were participating in a psychological experiment. When the amount of attitude change for these subjects was compared with that in a control group where the demand characteristics were not made so explicit, it was found that the experimental group of subjects had changed their attitudes in the recommended direction to a significantly greater extent than had the control subjects. In a similar vein, Adair and Schachter (1972) found that hypothesis-confirming behavior by subjects tends to increase when demand characteristics are made more pronounced so they can be more clearly and accurately perceived. However, perhaps the critical factor in whether the subject will guide his behavior according to his perceptions is his motivational set.

Step 3 is the subject's motivation pursuant to the demand characteristics of the situation. It has been shown that people who volunteer to be research subjects tend to be more acquiescent to demand characteristics than nonvoluntary subjects (Rosenthal and Rosnow, 1974), and there are several plausible explanations for this motivation. Cooperating with the researcher might be a self-justification for volunteering; or volunteering might be the foot in the door which opens the way to greater compliance; or perhaps there is a self-selection factor at work. The literature comparing willing and unwilling subjects suggests that volunteers may be characterized as better educated, higher in status, more approval seeking, less authoritarian, more sociable and arousal seeking, brighter, and younger individuals. These subjects' role behavior can be complicated, however, by the hints of what is expected in the research. When the demand characteristics are simple and straightforward but not patently obtrusive, volunteers may tend to be more compliant. At the other extreme, when the demands are not readily apparent, differences in the results between research on volunteers and research using nonvoluntary subjects may be quite negligible. To play good subject requires the desire *and* a knowledge of what is useful.

When the subject's need to present a favorable image is strongly in conflict with his desire to be useful, the situation can be further complicated. A case in point was a study by Sigall, Aronson, and Van Hoose (1970), in which two sets of cues were intended to operate simultaneously. One set of cues was related to the demand characteristics of the experiment, and the competing set conveyed the idea that compliance with demand characteristics would result in the subject being unfavorably evaluated on an important psychological dimension.

In this case, instead of cooperating with the experimenter by complying with demand characteristics, the subjects responded in the direction they would have seen as promoting a favorable self-image. No doubt there are other factors as well that can counteract a subject's initial positive motivation. If a subject felt that his freedom to act in whatever way he'd like were seriously restricted by the demand characteristics of the situation, this could arouse a strongly negative set. Anti-establishment attitudes could also be projected in countercompliant behavior. People with personality disorders—psychopathy and sociopathy, for example—should also be uncooperative research subjects. An unpleasant or highly temperamental experimenter, a subject whose suspicions had been aroused or who felt that he was being deceived by the researcher—these factors, too, might elicit a negative motivational set.

Step 4 is the subject's capability to respond pursuant to his motivations. Being biologically incapable of complying with demand characteristics should incapacitate even the most eager and aware of good subjects. Suppose, in an hypnosis experiment, that the task was to perform the "human plank trick," in which the hypnotized subject is suspended in midair with only his head and feet resting on supports. Even the most acquiescent volunteer must fail to comply with the experimenter's wish if the subject lacked the physical stamina required to perform this trick. Of course, this mediating stage in the role behavior of research subjects is one to which most behavioral scientists are intuitively and routinely attuned, and the experienced researcher would not think to select experimental circumstances that could be beyond the bounds of his subjects' normal capabilities. For this reason, the two most important mediating stages in actual practice are receptivity and motivation.

Step 5 is the subject's behavior, and it will be primarily operative through the combined mediation of steps 2 and 3. We need not pursue this combinatorial effect in detail, as the interested reader will find a full description of its theoretical operation elsewhere (cf. McGuire, 1968; Rosenthal and Rosnow, 1974). Suffice to say that this theory assumes that there is a trichotomy of mutually exclusive and exhaustive states of subject role behaviors—compliance with demand characteristics, noncompliance, and countercompliance—and that they are seen as the end products of the mediating stages in steps 2, 3, and 4.

Figure 3 shows the various sequences of these mediating stages, and it helps us to visualize the methodological problem of trying to cope with the biasing effects of observational reactivity. There are six branches shown in this tree diagram, all but paths 1 and 3 leading to behavior that could be free of reactive error. Path 1 leads to role behavior that is compliant with the demand characteristics of the situa-

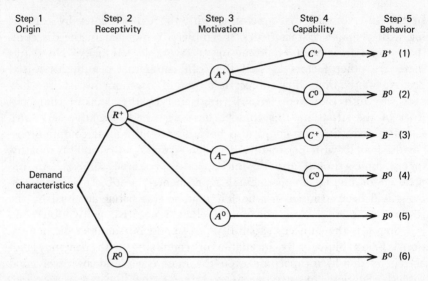

| Step 1 Origin | Step 2 Receptivity | Step 3 Motivation | Step 4 Capability | Step 5 Behavior |

FIGURE 3. A tree diagram to illustrate the sequences of mediating states leading to compliant behavior (B^+), noncompliant behavior (B°), and countercompliant behavior (B^-). The mediating states are designated as R^+ = adequate reception of demand characteristics; R° = inadequate reception; A^+ = acquiescent motivational set; A^- = counteracquiescent set; A° = nonacquiescent; C^+ = capable of responding to demand characteristics; C° = incapable of responding to demand characteristics.

tion; this would be a subject who perceived the researcher's wishes or expectations, was motivated in a positive direction, and was capable of playing the good subject role. Path 3 shows the opposite behavioral effect—the subject who is motivated in a negative direction. Paths 2 and 4 are limited by the capability state; path 5, by the subject's lack of motivation; and path 6, by the receptivity state. The methodological problem is either to circumvent the outcomes of paths 1 and 3 or to be able to partial out the amount of error operating in situations where the biasing effects of observational reactivity cannot be avoided. There are several alternative ways of coping with this problem within each of these two alternative modes .

ATTEMPTS AT CIRCUMVENTING OBSERVATIONAL REACTIVITY

Among the many interesting solutions to this problem that have been suggested are the use of more naturalistic realism when concocting experimental treatments (Aronson and Carlsmith, 1968), substitute procedures such as experimental role playing (cf. Kelman, 1972; Miller, 1972), greater use of laboratory deceptions or quasi-experimental designs in field settings (Campbell and Stanley, 1966; Cook and Campbell, 1974), guarantees of response anonymity for subjects (Rosnow, Holper, and Gitter, 1973; Webb, Campbell, Schwartz, and Sechrest, 1966, p. 15), and various other procedures (cf. Rosenthal and Rosnow, 1974). However, perhaps the most widely adopted means of trying to avoid this methodological difficulty is the technique of disguised experimentation in natural, nonlaboratory situations (Campbell, 1969). If the reactivity problem stems from the fact that subjects engage in artifactual behaviors in response to demand characteristics when they believe that a researcher is observing them, then one alternative solution is to shift the subject's attention away from the demand characteristics and refocus it on naturalistic social demands.

A classic illustration of this strategy was a study of the comparative effects of rational and emotional political propaganda carried out by George W. Hartmann during a statewide election campaign in Allentown, Pennsylvania in 1935. Hartmann, whose own name had been placed on the ballot as a Socialist party candidate, wrote two political leaflets, one of which was designed to appeal to the voters' reason and the other to their emotions. He then had the leaflets distributed in different wards that he matched on the basis of their size, population density, assessed property valuation, previous voting habits, and socioeconomic status. By comparing the election results in the wards that got the rational appeal versus those that got the emotional appeal, he deduced that the emotional propaganda must have had the stronger impact because the returns showed that this propaganda device was associated with greater increases in voting for the Socialist party relative both to the control regions and to increases in voting for Democratic and Republican candidates.

Another good example of field experimentation using disguised procedures was a cross-national research study on helping behavior that was conducted by Roy E. Feldman (1968). For many kinds of behavior, the cultural context in which the behavior is enacted can be an important variable. Feldman repeated several standard experiments in Athens, Paris, and Boston, using both foreigners and natives of the region as confederates. In one study he had the confederates ask directions from passersby; in another, they asked strangers to mail a letter for them, explaining that they were waiting for someone and couldn't leave the spot right then; in a third study, confederates overpaid merchants or taxi drivers and then observed whether the people were honest and returned the money. By cross-tabulating the results of the reactions of more than 3000 research subjects, Feldman was able to show that when a difference in helping behavior occurred, Parisians and Bostonians treated compatriots better than they did foreigners whereas Athenians were more helpful to foreigners than to compatriots.

Arguing for a greater utilization of unobtrusive measurements of dependent variables as another way of circumventing the problem of observational reactivity, Webb, Campbell, Schwartz, and Sechrest (1966) have provided a very useful discussion of these ingenious measures which can be triangulated in order to zero in on a behavioral response. Suppose we wanted to know the relative popularity of museum exhibits with glass fronts. We could interview people as they left the museum, but then we would run the risk of observational reactivity. Perhaps we could have inconspicuous research assistants keep a record of the number of people before each exhibit and the length of time each person spends there. That is a fairly time-consuming procedure, but it might be tried. If our observer were himself observed, we are back to the problem of reactivity, as the people might now spend more time in front of exhibits they felt would impress the observer. Perhaps we could dust the glass fronts each evening for noseprints. Exhibits having more noseprints on the glass may have been more, or at least more closely, observed. Distance of noseprints from the floor might even provide a crude index of the ages of the viewers. In addition to noseprint counting, we could keep track of the frequency with which it was necessary to replace the tiles in front of each exhibit.

Webb, Campbell, Schwartz, and Sechrest have other ingenious ideas. They suggest, for example, that if the effect of an airline disaster might be to increase travelers' anxiety levels, then good unobtrusive indices of this anxiety might include increased sales at airport bars, increased sales of trip insurance policies, and, of course, decreased sales of air travel tickets. Finally, they remind us of Richard LaPiere's (1934) classic research on prejudice. LaPiere and a Chinese couple visited over 200 hotels and restaurants and were refused service on only one occasion. Yet, of these same and comparable establishments, 9 out of 10 filled out questionnaires indicating they would *not* welcome Chinese customers. Here, then, was one of those unexpected cases where avowed discrimination was nearly unanimous while actual discrimination was virtually nonexistent.

The "bogus pipeline" is another recent effort to develop means of circumventing observational reactivity. Where disguised field research and the use of unobtrusive measures might be seen as a path 6 solution (in that demand characteristics are short-circuited at the receptivity stage), the bogus pipeline corresponds most closely to path 5. In this case, there is no attempt to turn the subject's attention away from the demand characteristics but to drain his motivation to respond pursuant to these cues and to give instead a more naturalistic sample of his behavior. Developed by Edward E. Jones and Harold Sigall (1971) as a way of assuring more objectively valid data by incorporating deception in the measurement of the dependent variable, the format is comparable to most self-rating attitude measures except that the subject is led to believe that a physiological monitoring device will catch him if he lies to the researcher. The methodology is still in the experimental stage of development, and its utility has recently been debated (Jones and Sigall, 1973; Ostrom, 1973). However, it provides an imaginative first step for dealing with this knotty problem.

ASSESSING THE EFFECTS OF OBSERVATIONAL REACTIVITY

Field research using unobtrusive measures of variables can be a very useful approach in the behavioral sciences, and it has begun to be widely used particularly among psychologists and sociologists who are experimentally inclined. However, the approach does not always permit the degree of precision that is afforded by laboratory research. For this reason, it is useful to have an arsenal of procedures for combating the effects of observational reactivity in laboratory experimentation. The bogus pipeline, used in conjunction with more routine attitude measurements, may be one way of assessing the effects of observational reactivity by comparing the responses of participants who were subjected to different measurement conditions. The measurement paradigm of "dual observation" proceeds on roughly the same idea and provides an alternative means of assessing the effects of observational reactivity when the problem is unavoidable (Rosnow and Aiken, 1973).

Dual observation is useful under the conditions shown by paths 1 and 3 in Figure 3. That is, the subject can be assumed to be role playing in response to demand characteristics, and the question is the direction and amount of bias on the dependent measure introduced by this effect of observational reactivity. In dual observation, the idea is to "reobserve" the original critical responses, perhaps outside the laboratory, in an atmosphere where the subject is not cognizant of whatever salient theoretical contingencies or experimental implications of his behavior may have affected his initial responding. This does not mean that he should be unaware of being observed, only that he does not connect the fact of his now being observed with the research or the researcher. The difference between observations, minus any nuisance variables, could provide an estimate of the invalidity which is a function of the totality of demand associated biases in the research setting and, by inference, in similar settings in past research.

To illustrate the practical use of dual observation, a clever application of this paradigm was in a study by Orne, Sheehan, and Evans (1968) on the effects of laboratory posthypnotic suggestion. Hypnotized subjects and a control group of subjects who simulated being hypnotized were given the suggestion that, for the next two days, every time they heard the word "experiment" mentioned, they would respond by touching their forehead. First the researchers tested the suggestion in the original experimental setting. Then, testing it again when the dominant situational contingencies were different, they had a secretary in the waiting room confirm the time of the subject's appointment "to come for the next part of the *experiment*." Later she asked the subject if she could pay him "now for today's *experiment* and for the next part of the study tomorrow." On the following day she met the subject with the question: "Are you here for Dr. Sheehan's *experiment*?"

Another procedure for probing the influence of subjects' role-play behavior is to incorporate an additional control group for this factor in the research design and then to compare the subjects' behaviors in the experimental group relative to the several control groups. Zimbardo, Marshall, White, and Maslach (1973) added this feature to a standard research design in another hypnosis experiment, this one on the effects of hypnotically induced time distortion. Before the experiment, one group of subjects (the experimental group) submitted to a 10-hour training program where they were taught to relax deeply and to induce autohypnosis. When the experiment began, this group was subjected to a state of hypnotic relaxation that was induced by a second experimenter. Of the two control groups used, one group (the hypnotic role players) was instructed by the same experimenter to try their best to simulate the reactions of hypnotized subjects. The other control group (the waking nonhypnotized controls) was told only to relax for the same period of time as the subjects in the other two groups. The dependent variable for all subjects was their facility at keeping a red light or a blue light illuminated by learning to push a control key at exactly the right tempo. The research design had elements of all three basic designs discussed in Chapter 4. That there were different treatment groups to which the subjects could be randomly assigned corresponds to the randomized research design. That the subjects in each group participated in a series of repeated learning trials corresponds to the treatments-by-subjects research design. To add a second dimension to the design, the lights remained functional during the experimental periods for half the subjects thus providing them with objective feedback on how well they were progressing, whereas for the other subjects in each treatment group the lights were extinguished, thus depriving them of any objective feedback. As an added fillip, all the subjects were intensively interviewed once the experiment was over in order to learn more about how they may have tried to satisfy the experimenter's demand to keep the target light illuminated, and a sub-group of the hypnotic role players was subsequently given the same program of hypnotic training that the experimental group had undergone and then retested with the hypnotic induction.

Few studies use such elaborate designs for assessing the effects of observational reactivity as in these two experiments. However, there are also easier procedures for getting at least a rough idea of the possible biasing influence of this complicated factor. Orne (1969) has suggested the use of "quasi-control" groups as a very general check on the effects of demand characteristics. His idea is to have subjects step out of their traditional role and to redefine the interaction between researcher and subject so as to make the subjects in a sense "co-investigators" rather than objects for the researcher to manipulate. Quasi-control subjects are drawn from the same population as the experimental subjects, but the quasi-controls clinically reflect upon the context in which the experiment is being conducted, and they speculate on ways in which it might influence their behavior if they were in the experimental group. While this simple procedure can provide only a very crude, qualitative estimate of the subjects' awareness of demand contingencies, when skillfully used in conjunction with the paradigm of dual observation the combined methodology should provide an effective test of the validity of inferences about the assumed relationships between variables.

INTERNAL AND EXTERNAL VALIDITY OF INFERENCES

The very business of science is to draw valid inferences about relationships between variables based on careful observations of nature. The importance of controls in the behavioral sciences stems from the fact that researchers have learned that invalid inferences about relationships are more likely when adequate controls are not employed. But it is possible to have a perfectly valid experiment leading to an inference that is invalid in the world at large. To explain this apparent paradox we draw on the ideas of two more kinds of validity to add to the list of those discussed in Chapter 5. These two new kinds, called internal and external validity, were first identified by Donald T. Campbell (cf. Campbell and Stanley, 1966; Webb, Campbell, et al., 1966).

An inference can be regarded as internally valid when the relationship claimed to have been found has indeed been found for that sample of observations on which the inference is based. Well-conducted experiments employing the principle of random assignment of subjects to treatment conditions tend to be valid internally although there are certain threats to internal validity even in the case of the formal experiment.

Suppose, for example, that a male and female student decide to conduct, as a team, an experiment on verbal learning. Their particular interest is in the effect of stress, in the form of loud noise, on the learning of prose material. In order to divide the work equitably, the experimenters flip a coin to determine which one of them will contact the subjects of the stress condition and which one will contact the subjects of the no-stress condition. Subjects are then assigned at random to one of the two conditions of the experiment. Suppose we find that better learning occurred in the stress condition. Can we ascribe the effect to the experimental stress? Probably not, because we have what Campbell has called a "plausible rival hypothesis" to the hypothesis of "result is due to stress." In this example, the plausible rival hypothesis is "result is due to sex of experimenter." This particular plausible rival hypothesis could have been fairly well ruled out in this specific experiment by having each of the two experimenters contact half the subjects of the experimental condition and half the subjects of the control condition. Such a plan would avoid the confounding or intermixing of the effects of stress and the effects of the experimenter's sex.

In the case of internal validity we were concerned only with the tenability of a particular set of observations made at one or more particular time periods, at one or more particular locales, using particular measuring instruments, particular data collectors, and particular subjects. Without internal validity we know nothing, but even with it we still may not know very much. If our internally valid experiment can never be replicated in other laboratories or by other investigators, or with other subjects, or with slightly different measuring instruments, then what we have learned may be true enough but is a truth that casts only a small spot of light. External validity, then, refers to the robustness of the truth or finding. An example may be useful. We said that it is known that people who volunteer to participate in behavioral experiments are different in a number of important ways from those who do not volunteer for such research participation. If an experiment were conducted employing a volunteer sample and the members of this sample were assigned at random to the various experimental conditions, we would have a good chance of achieving an internally valid result despite the nonrepresentativeness of the volunteer sample. The chances are, however, that the employment of such a different, or biased, or atypical sample, would give us little reason to hope for much in the way of external validity.

This brings us back to a significant point brought out in Chapter 3, which is the importance of well-conceived systematic replications in a carefully designed program of behavioral research. There is no better procedure for assuring the internal and external validity of inferred relationships than to retest them using multiple research methodologies, using different controls depending on the variations of independent and dependent variables that are operating, and to probe the effects on different populations of research subjects. If the external validity of a relationship can be jeopardized by the fact that it was established using only very highly motivated, volunteer subjects, then a way of proving its robustness would be to replicate the findings using a more representative population of subjects. It is incumbent upon the good researcher to use the very best procedures he can for assuring the internal validity of his findings and for showing the limits to the obtained relationships between variables.

chapter seven

ethical issues

OPENNESS IN BEHAVIORAL RESEARCH

Imagine an experiment in which the experimenter greeted his subjects by saying "Hello, today we are going to investigate the effects of physical distance from the victim on willingness to inflict pain on him. You will be in the 'close' condition, which means that you are expected to be somewhat less ruthless. In addition, you will be asked to fill out a test of fascist tendencies because we believe there is a positive relationship between scores on our fascism test and obedience to an authority who requests that we hurt others. Any questions?"

A completely honest statement to a research subject of what he is doing in an experiment might involve a prebriefing of the kind given. Such a prebriefing is manifestly absurd if we are serious in our efforts to learn about human behavior. If subjects had full information about our experimental plans, procedures and hypotheses, we might very well develop a psychology based on what subjects thought the world was like or what subjects thought experimenters thought the world was like. Subjects' knowledge of or suspicions about the purpose of the research (McGuire, 1969), coupled with their tendency to want to be good subjects (Orne, 1969; Rosnow, 1970) and to "look good" in the eyes of the experimenter (Rosenberg, 1969), constitutes a special case of the more general problem of observational reactivity just discussed.

The problem of subjects' knowledge of the true intent of the experiment is sufficiently threatening to the internal validity of the research, that behavioral scientists have almost routinely employed one form or another of deception of subjects. There are few behavioral researchers who advocate the use of deception in and of itself. At the same time, there are few researchers who feel that we can do entirely without deception. No one seriously advocates giving up the study of racial prejudice and discrimination. Yet, if all measures of racial prejudice had to be accurately labeled as such, it is questionable that it would be worth the effort to continue the research.

To adopt a rigid moralistic orientation requires that a deception be labeled a deception and that by our dominant value system, which decries deception at least in a formal sense, it be banished or ruled out. In fact, most people, including behavioral scientists, are willing to weigh and measure their sins, judging some to be larger than others. In the case of deceptions, fairly good agreement could probably be obtained on the proposition that refraining from telling a subject that an experiment in the learning of verbal materials is designed to show whether earlier, later, or more-midmost material is better remembered is not a particularly serious breach of ethical standards. The reason we do not view this deception with alarm seems due in part to its involving a sin of omission rather than commission. A truth is left unspoken, a lie is not told. Suppose, however, that the same experiment were presented as a study of the effects of meaningfulness of verbal material on its retention or recall. That is a direct lie, designed to mislead the subject's attention from the temporal order of the material to some other factor in which we really are not interested. Somehow, that change does not seem to make the deception so much more heinous even though now our sin is of commission and we have not withheld information from, but actively lied to, our subject.

It does not seem, then, that the style of the deception is its measure but, instead, its probable effect on the subject. Very few people would care whether subjects focused on meaningfulness of verbal material rather than temporal order since there seems to be no consequence, positive or negative, of this deception. It seems that it is not deception so much as it is harmful deception that we would like to minimize, and that it is the degree of harmfulness on which we can agree fairly well. Most people would agree that it is not very harmful to subjects to be told that a test they are taking anonymously as part of the research is one of personal reactions (which it is) rather than a test of need for social approval, schizophrenic tendencies, or authoritarianism (which it may also be). On the other hand, most people would probably agree that it could be harmful to college-age subjects to be falsely told that a test shows them to be homosexual even if they are later told they had been lied to. Most people would probably also agree that it may well be harmful to army recruits to be led to believe that they are in a stricken airplane about to crash, or that they have inadvertently killed some army buddies and that, to be able to report this, they had to repair a broken telephone ("the effect of stress on the performance of technical duties").

Some of the potentially most harmful deceptions, perhaps, ought never to be employed but, then, they are quite rare in any case. For the great bulk of deceptions where there may be a range of potentially negative consequences, the investigator, his colleagues, and to some extent, ultimately, the general community, must decide whether a deception of a given degree of potential negative effects is worth the potential increase in knowledge. There has been increasing discussion in recent years about the ethical problems raised here including thoughtful consideration put forward by Campbell (1969), Kelman (1972), and McGuire (1969). There has also been some interest in showing empirically the ethical dilemma facing the behavioral scientist who wishes to be open and straightforward with his research subjects but realizes that to reveal the substance of his research might jeopardize the internal validity of the findings.

THE RESNICK AND SCHWARTZ STUDY

You will recall in Chapter 2 our discussion of a series of verbal conditioning studies carried out by Crowne and Marlowe in developing their scale of social desirability (see pp. 27 ff.). A more recent experiment using this paradigm was by Jerome H. Resnick and his student, Thomas Schwartz (1973), to study empirically the effects of openness as an independent variable in behavioral research.

This particular experimental paradigm, in which the experimenter shapes the subject's utterances by saying "good" or "mmm-hmmm" or "okay" every time the subject gives the desired verbal response, has been used in more than 400 studies to explore a wide range of psychological behaviors. In Resnick and Schwartz's verbal conditioning study, the subject and the experimenter were seated at opposite sides of a table across which the experimenter passed a series of 3 × 5 inch cards to the subject one at a time. A different verb and six pronouns (I, WE, YOU, THEY, SHE, HE) were printed on each card, and the subject's instructions were to construct a sentence containing the verb and any one of the six pronouns. By rewarding the subject with verbal approval ("good" or "okay") each time a sentence was begun with I or WE, the experimenter could study the rate at which the subject learned to make the correct I and WE responses. To provide a standard by which to gauge how well each subject was progressing, on the first 20 trials the experimenter remained silent. In this way, the subject, by revealing what his base-rate of verbal behavior was like when the experimenter wasn't trying to condition him, could then serve as his own control in the experiment proper when the verbal conditioning trials were started. These verbal conditioning trials, of which there were 80, followed immediately upon completion of the 20 base-rate trials. To determine the effects of openness, the subjects were randomly assigned to either of two groups. In one group, the experimenter was completely open with them on the purpose, explicit procedure, and expected results of the study. In the other group, he was not; for these subjects, the only information they received concerned the general format of the experimental procedure.

Resnick and Schwartz's findings may not come as a surprise. For the uninformed group, the conditioning results were exactly as other investigators had shown, time and again, and that have provided some of the basis of our current laws of verbal learning. In essence, they showed that the experimenter's use of verbal reinforcements tended to facilitate the construction of I, WE sentences. For the fully informed group, the results were just the opposite. Instead of playing the good subject role, these subjects responded counter to demand characteristics; several of them mentioned to the experimenter that they suspected an elaborate double-reverse manipulation! Imagine what our science of verbal learning would look like if this prebriefing procedure had been naively used in all those hundreds of verbal conditioning studies. Resnick and Schwartz's findings are important in emphasizing the complexity of the ethical dilemma facing the conscientious behavioral scientist who, confronted with a conflict of values, must weigh the social ethic against the scientific ethic and decide which violation constitutes the lesser evil. Fortunately, there are some useful principles to turn to in helping to make this decision.

ETHICAL PRINCIPLES IN THE CONDUCT OF BEHAVIORAL RESEARCH

After a long period of study and much debate, the American Psychological Association published in 1973 a set of ethical guidelines that had been adopted the previous year by their council of representatives. These ten principles emphasize certain human guarantees that should weigh in the behavioral scientist's considered judgment about how best to contribute to science and to human welfare. The code recognizes that in each case there are balancing considerations for and against research that raises ethical issues, and the 1973 monograph is replete with examples to help the researcher choose the most humane and scientifically efficacious alternative methodology. The code recognizes also that we researchers may not always be the most objective judges of the pros and cons of our own research when it raises an ethical question. Because personal involvement can blind even a very conscientious researcher, it is wise to consult with others on one's individual responsibility. Most American colleges and universities, cognizant of the ethical dilemma in human scientific research, have committees that can be sought out in this advisory capacity, and the logical first step for the student who is involved with his own scientific project will be to consult with an experienced faculty advisor on the social and scientific alternatives available to him.

These ten principles make explicit the scientist's ethical responsibilities toward his research subjects over the entire course of the research. Read without any interstitial commentary, they might seem to be putting an end to any but the most open of projects. However, this is certainly not meant to be the case, as, from what Resnick and Schwartz's experiment teaches, the implications of such a policy might be disastrous for behavioral science. Hence, it is important to interpret each principle within the context of the various scientific and humane issues that are involved. The student who is about to embark on a research project would do well to familiarize himself with the thoughtful contents of this important monograph after he has studied the substantive literature in the area of his project but before he is committed to a particular research approach and methodology. This 100-page booklet should be available in most psychology departmental libraries, and it can also be obtained by writing directly to the American Psychological Association (1200 Seventeenth Street, N.W., Washington, D. C. 20036) and requesting information on their monograph entitled, "Ethical Principles in the Conduct of Research with Human Participants." We conclude by reprinting, with permission of the American Psychological Association, the ten ethical principles.

1. In planning a study the investigator has the personal responsibility to make a careful evaluation of its ethical acceptability, taking into account these Principles for research with human beings. To the extent that this appraisal, weighing scientific and humane values, suggests a deviation from any Principle, the investigator incurs an increasingly serious obligation to seek ethical advice and to observe more stringent safeguards to protect the rights of the human research participant.

2. Responsibility for the establishment and maintenance of acceptable ethical practice in research always remains with the individual investigator. The investigator is also responsible for the ethical treat-

ment of research participants by collaborators, assistants, students, and employees, all of whom, however, incur parallel obligations.

3. Ethical practice requires the investigator to inform the participant of all features of the research that reasonably might be expected to influence willingness to participate and to explain all other aspects of the research about which the participant inquires. Failure to make full disclosure gives added emphasis to the investigator's responsibility to protect the welfare and dignity of the research participant.

4. Openness and honesty are essential characteristics of the relationship between investigator and research participant. When the methodological requirements of a study necessitate concealment or deception, the investigator is required to ensure the participant's understanding of the reasons for this action and to restore the quality of the relationship with the investigator.

5. Ethical research practice requires the investigator to respect the individual's freedom to decline to participate in research or to discontinue participation at any time. The obligation to protect this freedom requires special vigilance when the investigator is in a position of power over the participant. The decision to limit this freedom in creases the investigator's responsibility to protect the participant's dignity and welfare.

6. Ethically acceptable research begins with the establishment of a clear and fair agreement between the investigator and the research participant that clarifies the responsibilities of each. The investigator has the obligation to honor all promises and commitments included in that agreement.

7. The ethical investigator protects participants from physical and mental discomfort, harm, and danger. If the risk of such consequences exists, the investigator is required to inform the participant of that fact, secure consent before proceeding, and take all possible measures to minimize distress. A research procedure may not be used if it is likely to cause serious and lasting harm to participants.

8. After the data are collected, ethical practice requires the investigator to provide the participant with a full clarification of the nature of the study and to remove any misconceptions that may have arisen. Where scientific or humane values justify delaying or withholding information, the investigator acquires a special responsibility to assure that there are no damaging consequences for the participant.

9. Where research procedures may result in undesirable consequences for the participant, the investigator has the responsibility to detect and remove or correct these consequences, including, where relevant, long-term aftereffects.

10. Information obtained about the research participants during

the course of an investigation is confidential. When the possibility exists that others may obtain access to such information, ethical research practice requires that this possibility, together with the plans for protecting confidentiality, be explained to the participants as a part of the procedure for obtaining informed consent.

references

Adair, J. G. & Schachter, B. S. To cooperate or to look good?: the subjects' and experimenters' perceptions of each others' intentions. *Journal of Experimental Social Psychology,* 1972, **8,** 74-85.

Allport, G. W., Bruner, J. S., & Jandorf, E. M. Personality under social catastrophes: ninety life histories of the Nazi revolution. In C. Kluckhohn and H. A. Murray (Eds.), *Personality: in nature, society, and culture.* (2nd ed.) New York: Knopf, 1953. Pp. 436-455.

Allport, G. W. & Postman, L.J. *The psychology of rumor.* New York: Holt, Rinehart & Winston, 1947.

Aronson, E. & Carlsmith, J. M. Experimentation in social psychology. In G. Lindzey & E. Aronson (Eds.), *The handbook of social psychology.* (Rev. ed., Vol. 2.) Reading, Mass.: Addison-Wesley, 1968. Pp. 1-79.

Asch, S. E. *Social psychology.* Englewood Cliffs, N. J.: Prentice-Hall, 1952.

Barber, B. Resistance by scientists to scientific discovery. *Science,* 1961, **134,** 596-602.

Bavelas, A. Communication patterns in task-oriented groups. *Journal of the Acoustical Society of America,* 1950, **22,** 725-730.

Beez, W. V. Influence of biased psychological reports on teacher behavior and pupil performance. *Proceedings of the 76th Annual Convention of the American Psychological Association,* 1968, 605-606.

Boder, D. P. *I did not interview the dead.* Urbana: University of Illinois Press, 1949.

Boring, E. G. Perspective: artifact and control. In R. Rosenthal & R. L.

Rosnow (Eds.), *Artifact in behavioral research*. New York: Academic Press, 1969, Pp. 1-11.

Bresnahan, J. L. & Shapiro, M. M. A general equation and technique for the exact partitioning of chi-square contingency tables. *Psychological Bulletin*, 1966, **66**, 252-262.

Campbell, D. T. Prospective: artifact and control. In R. Rosenthal & R. L. Rosnow (Eds.), *Artifact in behavioral research*. New York: Academic Press, 1969. Pp. 351-382.

Campbell, D. T. & Stanley, J. C. *Experimental and quasi-experimental designs for research*. Chicago: Rand McNally, 1966.

Castellan, N. J., Jr. On the partitioning of contingency tables. *Psychological Bulletin*, 1965, **64**, 330-338.

Caws, P. The structure of discovery. *Science*, 1969, **166**, 1375-1380.

Cohen, J. *Statistical power analysis for the behavioral sciences*. New York: Academic Press, 1969.

Collins, B. E. & Raven, B. H. Group structure: attraction, coalitions, communication, and pover. In G. Lindzey & E. Aronson (Eds.), *The handbook of social psychology*. (Rev. ed., Vol. 4) Reading, Mass.: Addison-Wesley, 1969. Pp. 102-204.

Cook, T. D. & Campbell, D. T. The design and conduct of quasi-experiments and true experiments in field settings. In M. D. Dunnette (Ed.), *Handbook of industrial and organizational psychology*, 1974, Chic.: Rand-McNally (in press).

Cooper, J., Eisenberg, L., Robert, J., & Dohrenwend, B. S. The effect of experimenter expectancy and preparatory effort on belief in the probable occurrence of future events. *Journal of Social Psychology*, 1967, **71**, 221-226.

Corrozi, J. F. & Rosnow, R. L. Consonant and dissonant communications as positive and negative reinforcements in opinion change. *Journal of Personality and Social Psychology*, 1968, **8**, 27-30.

Crowne, D. P. & Marlowe, D. *The approval motive: studies in evaluative dependence*. New York: Wiley, 1964.

Dabbs, J. M. & Janis, I. L. Why does eating while reading facilitate opinion change?—an experimental inquiry. *Journal of Experimental Social Psychology*, 1965, **1**, 133-144.

Devore, I. & Hall, K. R. L. Baboon ecology. In I. DeVore, ed., *Primate behavior*. New York: Holt, Rinehart & Winston, 1965, Pp. 20-52.

Doob, A. N., Carlsmith, J. M., Freedman, J. L., Landauer, T. K., & Tom, S., Jr. Effect of initial selling price on subsequent sales. *Journal of Personality and Social Psychology*, 1969, **11**, 345-350.

Dollard, J., Doob, L. W., Miller, N. E., Mowrer, O. H., Sears, R. R. (Ford, C. S., Hovland, C. I., & Sollenberger, R. T.). *Frustration and aggression*. New Haven: Yale University Press, 1939.

Epstein, Y. M., Suedfeld, P., & Silverstein, S. J. The experimental contract: subjects' expectations of and reactions to some behaviors of experimenters. *American Psychologist,* 1973, **28**, 212-221.

Eron, L. D., Huessman, L. R., Lefkowitz, M. M., & Walder, L. O. Does television violence cause aggression? *American Psychologist,* 1972, **27**, 253-263.

Feldman, R. E. Response to compatriot and foreigner who seek assistance. *Journal of Personality and Social Psychology,* 1968, **10**, 202-214.

Festinger, L. *A theory of cognitive dissonance.* Evanston, Illinois: Row, Peterson, 1957.

Fillenbaum, S. Recall for answers to "conducive" questions. *Language and Speech,* 1968, **11**, 46-53.

Firth, R. Rumor in a primitive society. *Journal of Abnormal and Social Psychology,* 1956, **53**, 122-132.

Foa, U. G. Three kinds of behavioral change. *Psychological Bulletin,* 1968, **70**, 460-473.

Foa, U. G. Interpersonal and economic resources. *Science,* 1971, **171**, 345-351.

Foa, U. G. & Foa, E. B. *Societal structures of the mind.* Springfield, Ill.: Chas. Thomas, 1974.

Freedman, J. L. & Fraser, S. C. Compliance without pressure: the foot-in-the-door technique. *Journal of Personality and Social Psychology,* 1966, **4**, 195-202.

Gillig, P. M., & Greenwald, A. G. Is it time to lay the sleeper effect to rest? *Journal of Personality and Social Psychology,* 1974, **29**, 132-139.

Goffman, E. On face-work: an analysis of ritual elements in social interaction. *Psychiatry: Journal for the Study of Interpersonal Processes,* 1955, **18**, 213-231.

Goffman, E. Embarrassment and social organization. *American Journal of Sociology,* 1956, **62**, 264-274. (a)

Goffman, E. The nature of deference and demeanor. *American Anthropologist,* 1956, **58**, 473-502. (b)

Goffman, E. Alienation from interaction. *Human Relations,* 1957, **10**, 47-59.

Goldstein, J. H. & Arms, R. L. Effects of observing athletic contests on hostility. *Sociometry,* 1971, **34**, 83-90.

Harlow, H. F. Love in infant monkeys. In S. Coopersmith (Ed.), *Frontiers of psychological research.* San Francisco: W. H. Freeman, 1959, 1966, Pp. 92-98.

Harlow, H. F. & Harlow, M. K. The affectional systems. In A. M. Schrier, H. F. Harlow, & F. Stollnitz (Eds.), *Behavior of nonhuman primates: modern research trends.* (Vol. 2.) New York: Academic Press, 1965. Pp. 287-334.

Harlow, H. F. & Harlow, M. Learning to love. *American Scientist,* 1966, **54,** 244-272.

Harlow, H. F. & Harlow, M. The young monkeys. In P. Cramer (Ed.), *Readings in developmental psychology today.* Del Mar, Cal.: CRM Books, 1970. Pp. 93-97.

Hartmann, G. W. A field experiment on the comparative effectiveness of "emotional" and "rational" political leaflets in determining election results. *Journal of Abnormal and Social Psychology,* 1936, **31,** 99-114.

Higbee, K. L. & Wells, M. G. Some research trends in social psychology during the 1960s. *American Psychologist,* 1972, **27,** 963-966.

Hovland, C. I., Lumsdaine, A. A., & Sheffield, F. D. *Experiments on mass communication.* Princeton, N. J.: Princeton University Press, 1949.

Hovland, C. I. & Weiss, W. The influence of source credibility on communication effectiveness. *Public Opinion Quarterly,* 1951, **15,** 635-650.

Huesmann, L. R., Eron, L. D., Lefkowitz, M. M., & Walder, L. O. Television violence and aggression: the causal effect remains. *American Psychologist,* 1973, **28,** 617-620.

Janis, I. L., Kaye, D., & Kirschner, P. Facilitating effects of "eating-while-reading" on responsiveness to persuasive communications. *Journal of Personality and Social Psychology,* 1965, **1,** 181-186.

Janis, I. L., Lumsdaine, A. A., & Gladstone, A. I. Effects of preparatory communications on reactions to a subsequent news event. *Public Opinion Quarterly,* 1951, **15,** 487-518.

Jones, E. E. & Sigall, H. The bogus pipeline: a new paradigm for measuring affect and attitude. *Psychological Bulletin,* 1971, **76,** 349-364.

Jones, E. E. & Sigall, H. Where there is *ignis,* there may be fire. *Psychological Bulletin,* 1973, **79,** 260-262.

Jones, F. P. Experimental method in antiquity. *American Psychologist,* 1964, **19,** 419.

Jones, R. A. & Cooper, J. Mediation of experimenter effects. *Journal of Personality and Social Psychology,* 1971, **20,** 70-74.

Juday, R. E. Versatile genius: Frederick II. *Science,* 1968, **162,** 850-851.

Jung, C. G. Ein Beitrag zur Psychologie des Gerüchtes. *Zentralblatt für Psychoanalyse,* 1910, **1,** 81-90.

Jung, C. G. A visionary rumour. *Journal of Analytical Psychology,* 1959, **4,** 5-19.

Kelman, H. C. The rights of the subject in social research: an analysis in terms of relative power and legitimacy. *American Psychologist,* 1972, **27,** 989-1016.

Kenny, D. A. Threats to the internal validity of a cross-lagged panel inference, as related to "Television Violence and Child Aggression: A Follow-up

Study." In G. A. Comstock and E. A. Rubinstein (Eds.), *Television and social behavior*, Vol. 3. *Television and adolescent aggressiveness*. Wash., D. C.: U. S. Government Printing Office, 1972.

Lana, R. E. & Rosnow, R. L. *Introduction to contemporary psychology*. New York: Holt, Rinehart & Winston, 1972.

LaPiere, R. T. Attitudes vs. actions. *Social Forces*, 1934, **13**, 230-237.

Latané, B. & Darley, J. M. *The unresponsive bystander: why doesn't he help?* New York: Appleton-Century-Crofts, 1970.

Leavitt, H. J. Some effects of certain communication patterns on group performance. *Journal of Abnormal and Social Psychology*, 1951, **46**, 38-50.

Lessac, M. S. & Solomon, R. L. Effects of early isolation on the later adaptive behavior of beagles. *Developmental Psychology*, 1969, **1**, 14-25.

Lovell, B. Serendipity in science. *The London Times Educational Supplement*. December 12, 1972.

Lumsdaine, A. A. & Janis, I. L. Resistance to "counter-propaganda" produced by one-sided and two-sided "propaganda" presentations. *Public Opinion Quarterly*, 1953, **17**, 311-318.

Maslow, A. H. *Toward a psychology of being*. New York: Van Nostrand, 1962.

Matarazzo, J. D., Wiens, A. N., & Saslow, G. Studies in interview speech behavior. In L. Krasner and L. P. Ullman (Eds.), *Research in behavior modification*. New York: Holt, Rinehart and Winston, 1965. Pp. 179-210.

McClelland, D. C. *The achieving society*. Princeton: Van Nostrand, 1961 .

McGuire, W. J. Inducing resistance to persuasion: some contemporary approaches .In L. Berkowitz (Ed.), *Advances in Exeprimental social psychology*. Vol. 1. New York: Academic Press, 1964. Pp. 191-229.

McGuire, W. J. Personality and susceptibility to social influence. In E. F. Borgatta and W. W. Lambert (Eds.), *Handbook of personality theory and research*. Chicago, Rand McNally, 1968.

McGuire, W. J. Suspiciousness of experimenter's intent. In R. Rosenthal & R. L. Rosnow (Eds.), *Artifact in behavioral research*. New York: Academic Press, 1969. Pp. 13-57.

McGuire, W. J. The yin and yang of progress in social psychology: seven koan. *Journal of Personality and Social Psychology*, 1973, **26**, 446-456.

McNemar, Q. Opinion-attitude methodology. *Psychological Bulletin*, 1946, **43**, 289-374.

Merton, R. K. *Social theory and social structure* (Enlarged edition) New York: Free Press, 1968

Milgram, S. Behavioral study of obedience. *Journal of Abnormal and Social Psychology*, 1963, **67**, 371-378.

Milgram, S. Some conditions of obedience and disobedience to authority. *Human Relations*, 1965, **18**, 57-76.

Milgram, S. The experience of living in cities. *Science,* 1970, **167,** 1461-1468.

Miller, A. G. Role playing: an alternative to deception? *American Psychologist,* 1972, **27,** 623-636.

Miller, N. & Campbell, D. T. Recency and primacy in persuasion as a function of the timing of speeches and measurements. *Journal of Abnormal and Social Psychology,* 1959, **59,** 1-9.

Mosteller, F. Association and estimation in contingency tables. *Journal of the American Statistical Association,* 1968, **63,** 1-28.

Nisbett, R. E. Determinants of food intake in obesity. *Science,* 1968, **159,** 1254-1255.

Orne, M. T. On the social psychology of the psychological experiment: with particular reference to demand characteristics and their implications. *American Psychologist,* 1962, **17,** 776-783.

Orne, M. T. Demand characteristics and the concept of quasi-controls. In R. Rosenthal & R. L. Rosnow (Eds.), *Artifact in behavioral research.* New York: Academic Press, 1969. Pp. 143-179.

Orne, M. T., Sheehan, P. W., & Evans, F. J. Occurrence of posthypnotic behavior outside the experimental setting. *Journal of Personality and Social Psychology,* 1968, **9,** 189-196.

OSS Assessment Staff. *Assessment of men: selection of personnel for the Office of Strategic Services.* New York: Rinehart, 1948.

Ostrom, T. M. The bogus pipeline: a new *ignis fatuus? Psychological Bulletin,* 1973, **79,** 252-259.

Paine, R. Lappish decisions, partnerships, information management, and sanctions—a nomadic pastoral adaptation, *Ethnology,* 1970, **9,** 52-67.

Palardy, J. M. What teachers believe—what children achieve. *Elementary School Journal,* 1969, **69,** 370-374.

Platt, J. R. Strong inference. *Science,* 1964, **146,** 347-353.

Resnick, J. H. & Schwartz, T. Ethical standards as an independent variable in psychological research. *American Psychologist,* 1973, **28,** 134-139.

Rosenberg, M. J. The conditions and consequences of evaluation apprehension. In R. Rosenthal & R. L. Rosnow (Eds.), *Artifact in behavioral research.* New York: Academic Press, 1969. Pp. 279-349.

Rosenthal, A. M. *Thirty-six witnesses.* New York: McGraw-Hill, 1964.

Rosenthal, R. *Experimenter effects in behavioral research.* New York: Appleton-Century-Crofts, 1966.

Rosenthal, R. Covert communication in the psychological experiment. *Psychological Bulletin,* 1967, **67,** 356-367.

Rosenthal, R. Interpersonal expectations: effects of the experimenter's hypotheses. In R. Rosenthal & R. L. Rosnow (Eds.), *Artifact in behavioral research.* New York: Academic Press, 1969. Pp. 181-277.

Rosenthal, R. Estimating effective reliabilities in studies that employ judges' ratings. *Journal of Clinical Psychology*. 1973, **29**, 342-345. (a)

Rosenthal, R. On the social psychology of the self-fulfilling prophecy: further evidence for Pygmalion effects and their mediating mechanisms. In M. Kling (Ed.), *Reading and school achievement: cognitive and affective influences*. 8th Annual Spring Reading Conference, Rutgers University, 1973. (b)

Rosenthal, R. The Pygmalion effect. *Psychology Today*, 1973, **7**, 56-63. (c)

Rosenthal, R. & Jacobson, L. *Pygmalion in the classroom*. New York: Holt, Rinehart & Winston, 1968.

Rosenthal, R. & Rosnow, R. L. (Eds.) *Artifact in behavioral research*. New York: Academic Press, 1969.

Rosenthal, R. & Rosnow, R. L. *The volunteer subject*. New York: Wiley, 1974.

Rosnow, R. L. A "spread of effect" in attitude formation. In A. G. Greenwald, T. C. Brock, and T. M. Ostrom (Eds.), *Psychological foundations of attitudes*. New York: Academic Press, 1968. Pp. 89-107.

Rosnow, R. L. When he lends a helping hand, bite it. *Psychology Today*, 1970, **4** (1), 26-30.

Rosnow, R. L. Poultry and prejudice. *Psychology Today*, 1972, **5** (10), 53-56.

Rosnow, R. L. On rumor. *Journal of Communication*, 1974, **24** (3), 26-38.

Rosnow, R. L. & Aiken, L. S. Mediation of artifacts in behavioral research. *Journal of Experimental Social Psychology*, 1973, **9**, 181-201.

Rosnow, R. L. & Arms, R. L. Adding versus averaging as a stimulus-combination rule in forming impressions of groups. *Journal of Personality and Social Psychology*, 1968, **10**, 363-369.

Rosnow, R. L., Holper, H. M., & Gitter, A. G. More on the reactive effects of pretesting in attitude research: demand characteristics or subject commitment? *Educational and Psychological Measurement*, 1973, **33**, 7-17.

Rosnow, R. L., Wainer, H., & Arms, R. L. Personality and group impression formation as a function of the amount of overlap in evaluative meaning of the stimulus elements. *Sociometry*, 1970, **33**, 472-484 .

Rozelle, R. M. & Campbell, D. T. More plausible rival hypotheses in the cross-lagged panel correlation technique. *Psychological Bulletin*, 1969, **71**, 74-80.

Rozin, P. Specific aversions as a component of specific hungers. *Journal of Comparative and Physiological Psychology*, 1967, **64**, 237-242.

Rozin, P. Adaptive food sampling patterns in vitamin deficient rats. *Journal of Comparative and Physiological Psychology*, 1969, **69**, 126-132.

Schachter, S. *The psychology of affiliation: experimental studies of the sources of gregariousnes*. Stanford: Stanford University Press, 1959.

Schachter, S. & Burdick, H. A field experiment on rumor transmission and distortion. *Journal of Abnormal and Social Psychology,* 1955, **50**, 363-371.

Schultz, D. P. The human subject in psychological research. *Psychological Bulletin,* 1969, **72**, 214-228.

Shibutani, T. *Improvised news: a sociological study of rumor.* Indianapolis: Bobbs-Merrill, 1966.

Sigall, H., Aronson, E., & Van Hoose, T. The cooperative subject: myth or reality? *Journal of Experimental Social Psychology,* 1970, **6**, 1-10.

Silverman, I. Role-related behavior of subjects in laboratory studies of attitude change. *Journal of Personality and Social Psychology,* 1968, **8**, 343-348.

Skinner, B. F. *Beyond freedom and dignity.* New York: Alfred Knopf, 1971.

Skinner, B. F. *Cumulative Record* (3rd ed.) New York: Appleton-Century-Crofts, 1972.

Smart, R. G. Subject selection bias in psychological research. *Canadian Psychologist,* 1966, **7**, 115-121.

Solomon, R. L. An extension of control group design. *Psychological Bulletin,* 1949, **46**, 137-150.

Solomon, R. L. & Lessac, M. S. A control group design for experimental studies of developmental processes. *Psychological Bulletin,* 1968, **70**, 145-150.

Webb, E. J., Campbell, D. T., Schwartz, R. F., & Sechrest, L. *Unobtrusive measures: nonreactive research in the social sciences.* Chicago: Rand McNally, 1966.

Wilkins, L. & Richter, C. P. A great craving for salt by a child with corticoadrenal insufficiency. *Journal of the American Medical Association,* 1940, **114**, 866-868.

Zajonc, R. F. Social facilitation. *Science,* 1965, **149**, 269-274.

Zimbardo, P. G., Marshall, G., White G., & Maslach, C. Objective assessment of hypnotically induced time distortion. *Science,* 1973, **181**, 282-284.

index

113